EASY TRUE STORIES

A PICTURE-BASED BEGINNING READER

by Sandra Heyer

Longman

To the readers of this book, who tell the most amazing true stories of all.

Easy True Stories:
A Picture-Based Beginning Reader

Pearson Education, 10 Bank Street, White Plains, NY. 10606

Associated companies:
Longman Group Ltd., London
Longman Cheshire Pty., Melbourne
Longman Paul Pty., Auckland
Copp Clark Pitman, Toronto

Credits appear on page 91.

Distributed in the United Kingdom by Longman Group
Ltd., Longman House, Burnt Mill, Harlow, Essex CM20
2JE, England, and by associated companies, branches,
and representatives throughout the world.

Acquisitions director: Joanne Dresner
Senior development editor: Debbie Sistino
Production editor: Nik Winter
Text design: Carreiro Design
Text design adaptation: Pencil Point Studio
Cover design adaptation: Madkat Studio
Text art: Don Martinetti; Pencil Point Studio
Production supervisor: Richard Bretan

Library of Congress Cataloging in Publication Data

Heyer, Sandra.
    Easy true stories : a picture-based beginning reader / Sandra
Heyer.
        p.   cm.
    ISBN 0-8013-1089-X
    1. English language–Textbooks for foreign speakers. 2. Readers.
I. Title.
PE1128.H4355 1994
    428.6′4–dc20

                                                        93-34692
                                                        CIP

13 14 15 – VG – 02 01 00

Contents

Introduction

Easy True Stories is a beginning reader for students of English as a Second Language. It can be a first reader for students who have had some experience with English. The stories, written primarily in the present tense, are told in simple yet natural language.

Easy True Stores contains 20 units, each centered on a story that was adapted from a newspaper or magazine article. In answer to those students who think that some stories are too amazing to be true: Yes, the stories are true, to the best of our knowledge. All come from reputable news sources.

The advantage of basing the textbook on true stories is that real life provides stories that are often more gripping and more intriguing than those that come from an author's imagination. The disadvantage is that vocabulary and story length cannot be quite as rigidly controlled. To help students understand the new vocabulary and follow the story line, each unit of *Easy True Stories* includes a pre-reading page that tells the story in nine drawings. Following are some suggestions for using the pre-reading drawings and other elements of the units. Teachers new to the field might find the ideas especially helpful. Please remember that the suggestions are offered as exactly that: suggestions. Teachers should, of course, feel free to adapt these strategies to best meet their students' needs.

PRE-READING

Read the story aloud to students as they look at the drawings on the pre-reading page. Begin by saying "Number One" and slowly reading the sentences that the first picture illustrates. Then say "Number Two" and read the appropriate sentences. Continue in this manner. Saying the numbers of the pictures in the course of the story ensures that students are looking at the right picture.

Sometimes in reading the story aloud, you might want to break it down into even smaller chunks of meaning. In Unit 1, for example, the story begins, "Jim is looking out his window." Instead of reading this exactly as it is written, you might say, "The man's name is Jim. He is looking out his window." Breaking the story down into smaller pieces and pausing between the pieces gives students more time to digest the information.

Sometimes you'll need to digress from telling the story in order to clarify concepts and vocabulary. Again, Unit 1 provides an example. The second sentence of the story in Unit 1 — "He sees two men in his neighbor's driveway" — contains two words that are probably new: *neighbor* and *driveway*. You might go to the board and draw stick figures of Jim and his neighbor, their houses, garages, and driveways, verbally labeling the items as you draw. Then return to picture two of the story.

If you have access to an overhead projector, you could make transparencies of the pre-reading pages and show them this way, rather than having students follow in their textbooks. Then you can point to the drawings as you tell the story. With erasable markers, you can draw arrows to items, add drawings of your own, or write words next to the pictures.

After telling the story, you might want to check comprehension by reciting lines from the story and asking students to say the numbers of the corresponding pictures. Or, to bring students one step closer to reading, you could write key words on the board and ask students to say the numbers of the drawings in which those words are depicted. (To keep the atmosphere relaxed, call on the whole group for the answers, rather than on individuals.)

For most beginning students, the pre-reading activity is a crucial aid to understanding the written story. However, students who have had considerable experience with written English in their native countries but understand very little spoken English might benefit from reversing the procedure: reading the story first and *then* listening to it while looking at the pictures.

READING THE STORY

After listening to the story, students read the story silently. Students who finish reading before their classmates can go on to the exercises. Some students might want a little time to consult their bilingual dictionaries for the meanings of words that are still unclear.

In a beginning ESL class there is often a wide range of reading proficiency: Some students understand every word they read, while others get only the gist of the story. Assure students in the latter category that it is not essential to understand every word. The ability to be comfortable with a certain amount of ambiguity is a great asset to a beginning reader.

THE EXERCISES

Vocabulary and Comprehension. Each unit offers a variety of vocabulary and comprehension exercises. Use of the exercises can be tailored to the individual teaching environment and style. Students can work individually, in pairs, or in small groups. The exercises can be completed in class or assigned as homework. At the back of the book there is an answer key to the exercises.

Discussion. Some of the discussion exercises ask students to brainstorm to create lists. These activities are ideal for beginning students because they don't require students to produce whole sentences. Another advantage is that brainstorming activities can succeed without the whole class participating. Students who aren't ready to speak can listen and learn from the language their classmates and teacher produce.

Many of the discussion exercises ask students to respond to statements by circling *yes* or *no*. Some of the statements — such as "there are big snakes in my country" — invite further discussion. Some students will expand on their answers; others will simply answer the question. It is best not to make a big fuss over students' reticence. Beginning students need a "silent period" before they begin to speak, during which they try to make sense of the new language. Students who do not talk much may simply need a longer silent period than their more talkative classmates.

Writing. Most of the writing exercises will produce error-free writing; they are based on copying. Other writing exercises will result in writing that is not free from errors.

Some teachers may choose to correct the errors, while others may not; here teachers must use their own judgment.

The exercises are not included to make students struggle; choose exercises that your students can complete successfully. Both the exercises and reading selections are intended to build students' confidence along with their reading skills. Above all, it is hoped that reading *Easy True Stories* will be a pleasure, for both you and your students.

Easy True Stories is the first book in the *True Stories* reading series. It is followed by *True Stories in the News*, *More True Stories*, and *Even More True Stories*.

UNIT 1

1. PRE-READING

Look at the pictures. Listen to your teacher tell the story.

The Color TVs

JIM is looking out his window. He sees two men in his neighbor's driveway. The men are carrying a big color TV. They are carrying the TV to a truck.

Jim opens his window. "Hey!" he says to the two men. "Are you TV repairmen?"

"Yes," the men answer.

"Are you going to fix that TV?" Jim asks.

"Yes," the men answer again.

"My TV is broken," Jim tells the men. "Can you take my TV, too?"

"Sure," the men say. "We can take your TV."

Jim gives the men his color TV. The men put the two TVs in the truck and drive away.

Jim never sees his TV again.

The two men aren't TV repairmen. They are robbers.

2. VOCABULARY

Match the words and the pictures. Write your answer on the line.

5 neighbor   1 driveway   6 carry
7 fix   2 drive away   3 robber

1. _driveway_   2. _____   3. _____

4. _____   5. _____   6. _____

3. COMPREHENSION

REMEMBERING DETAILS

Which sentence is correct? Circle *a* or *b*.

1.   **a.**   Jim sees two cars in his neighbor's driveway.
      b.   Jim sees two men in his neighbor's driveway.

2.   **a.**   The men are carrying a big table.
      b.   The men are carrying a big color TV.

3.   **a.**   Jim asks the men, "Are you going to fix that TV?"
      b.   Jim asks the men, "Are you going to watch that TV?"

4.   **a.**   Jim tells the men, "My TV is broken."
      b.   Jim tells the men, "My TV is old."

5.   **a.**   The men put the TVs on the truck and pay Jim $25.
      b.   The men put the TVs on the truck and drive away.

REVIEWING THE STORY

Write the correct word on the line.

Jim sees two men in his _____*neighbor's*_____ driveway. The men are
1

_____ a big color TV. Jim thinks the men are TV
2

_____ . He gives them his color _____ .
3   4

Jim never sees his TV again because the men are _____ .
5

---

4. DISCUSSION

When robbers go into a house, what do they take? Money? Jewelry? Brainstorm with your classmates. Make a list of what you think robbers take. Your teacher will write your list on the blackboard.

Now turn to page 89. You will see a Robbers' List. Two hundred robbers answered the question: When you go into a house, what do you take? The robbers made a list. Look at the robbers' list. Are your list and their list the same?

---

5. WRITING

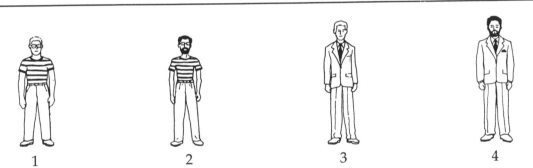

1   2   3   4

Choose one picture to write about. The man in the picture is a robber! Write four sentences about him. For example: He is thin. He has a beard. He wears glasses. He is wearing a suit.

1. _____

2. _____

3. _____

4. _____

Read your sentences to a classmate. Which robber did you write about? Can your classmate guess?

UNIT 2

Look at the pictures. Listen to your teacher tell the story.

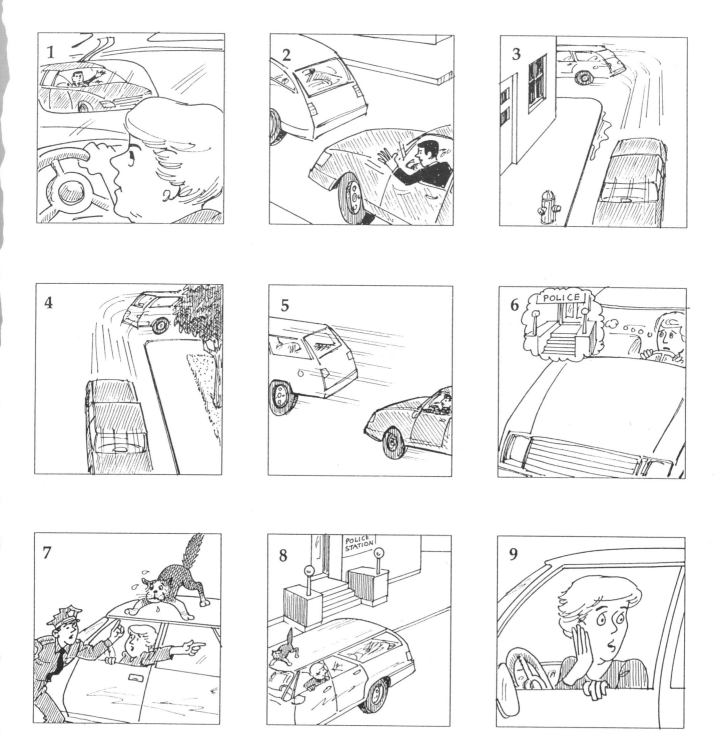

The Man in the Blue Car

MRS. Thompson is driving her car. She looks in the rearview mirror. A blue car is behind her. A man is driving the blue car.

The man in the blue car waves at Mrs. Thompson. He is saying something, but Mrs. Thompson can't hear him.

Mrs. Thompson turns left. The man in the blue car turns left, too.

Mrs. Thompson turns right. The man in the blue car turns right, too.

Mrs. Thompson drives fast. The man in the blue car drives fast, too.

Mrs. Thompson is afraid of the man in the blue car. She drives to the police station. The man in the blue car follows her.

Mrs. Thompson arrives at the police station and stops her car.

A police officer comes to Mrs. Thompson's car. The police officer says, ''There's a cat on the top of your car!''

Mrs. Thompson's cat is on the top of her car. The cat is *very* afraid.

Mrs. Thompson looks for the man in the blue car, but he is gone. Now Mrs. Thompson understands: The man in the blue car wanted to tell her, ''There's a cat on the top of your car!''

2. VOCABULARY

Match the words and the pictures. Write your answer on the line.

follow   top of the car   turn left
wave   afraid   rearview mirror

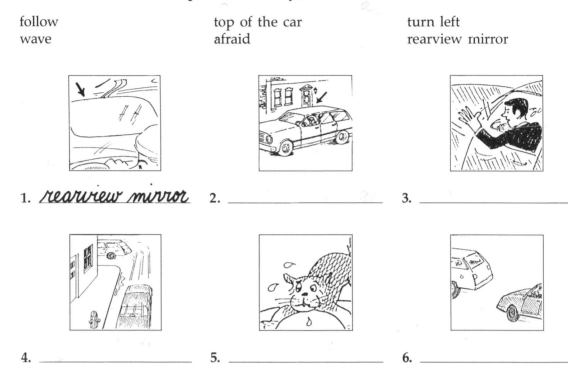

1. *rearview mirror*   2. _____   3. _____

4. _____   5. _____   6. _____

3. COMPREHENSION

REMEMBERING DETAILS

Which sentence is correct? Circle *a* or *b*.

1. a. Mrs. Thompson is driving her truck.
    (b.) Mrs. Thompson is driving her car.

2. a. A blue car is behind her.
    b. A black car is behind her.

3. a. The man in the car follows Mrs. Thompson.
    b. The man in the car likes Mrs. Thompson.

4. a. Mrs. Thompson drives home.
    b. Mrs. Thompson drives to the police station.

5. a. There is a man on the top of Mrs. Thompson's car.
    b. There is a cat on the top of Mrs. Thompson's car.

REVIEWING THE STORY

Write the correct word on the line.

A _____*man*_____ in a blue car follows Mrs. Thompson.
₁

Mrs. Thompson is _____ of the man. She drives to the
₂

_____ station. A police _____ tells her,
₃ ₄

" _____ a cat on the top of your car!" Mrs. Thompson looks
₅

for the man in the blue car, but he is _____ .
₆

---

4. DISCUSSION

Mrs. Thompson is driving with ten things on the top of her car. Look at the ten things for 30 seconds. Then close your book. How many things can you remember? With a small group of your classmates, make a list. Which group remembered all ten things?

---

5. WRITING

Mrs. Thompson wants to go to the police station. Here are directions to the police station. They are in the wrong order.
· Turn left on Sixth Street.
· Turn right on Fifth Street.
· The police station is on the right.
· Turn left on Park Avenue.
· Turn right on Center Street.

Copy the directions in the right order.

1. _*Turn right on Fifth Street.*_

2. _____

3. _____

4. _____

5. _____

1. PRE-READING

Look at the pictures. Listen to your teacher tell the story.

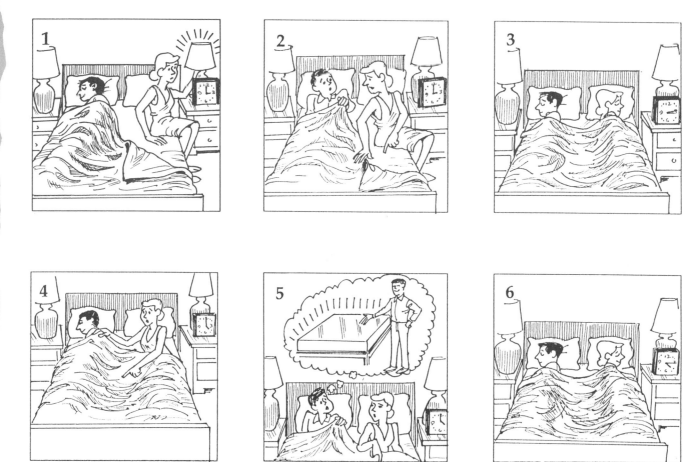

There's Something in the Mattress

IT is three o'clock in the morning. Gladys sits up in bed and turns on a light. "John! Wake up!" she tells her husband.

John wakes up and opens his eyes a little. "What's the matter?" he asks Gladys.

"Something is moving in the mattress," Gladys says. "There! It's moving now! Do you feel it?"

"No, I don't," John says. "I'm going back to sleep."

John and Gladys go back to sleep.

An hour later Gladys wakes up. "John!" she says. "It's moving again!"

"Gladys," John says, "this is a new mattress. There is nothing in the mattress."

John and Gladys go back to sleep again.

An hour later John jumps out of bed and turns on a light. "Something is moving in the mattress!" he says.

"You see!" Gladys says. "There *is* something in the mattress! Let's cut the mattress open."

"Cut our new mattress?" John asks.

"Yes," Gladys says. "I want to see inside."

John and Gladys cut the mattress open. Inside the mattress, they find a snake.

2. VOCABULARY

Write the opposites. You can find the words in the story.

1. turn off   t u r n   o n

2. go to sleep   w a k e   u

3. wife   a

4. a lot   t

5. old   n   w

6. something   o

7. close   p

8. outside   s

3. COMPREHENSION

MAKING CONNECTIONS

Find the best way to complete each sentence. Write the letter of your answer on the line.

1. Gladys sits up in bed and turns on __d__   **a.** a snake.

2. John wakes up and opens _____   **b.** the mattress.

3. Gladys tells her husband, _____   **c.** his eyes.

4. John and Gladys cut _____   **d.** a light.

5. Inside the mattress they find _____   **e.** "Something is moving in the mattress!"

REMEMBERING DETAILS

One word in each sentence is not correct. Find the word and cross it out. Write the correct word.

1. It is three o'clock in the ~~afternoon~~. *morning*

2. Gladys sits up in bed and turns off a light.

3. Gladys sees something in the mattress.

4. She tells John, "Something is sleeping in the mattress!"

5. John says, "The mattress is old; there is nothing in the mattress."

4. DISCUSSION

Circle *yes* or *no*.

In small groups, show your answers to your classmates. Are your answers and your classmates' answers the same? If you have a true story about a snake, tell the story to your classmates.

1. There are big snakes in my native country. (How big? Show your classmates with your hands.)   YES   NO

2. Snakes in my native country sometimes kill people.   YES   NO

3. I like snakes.   YES   NO

4. I am afraid of snakes.   YES   NO

5. I have a true story about a snake.   YES   NO

5. WRITING

Copy your *yes* sentences from the discussion exercise.

_____

_____

_____

_____

_____

1. PRE-READING

Look at the pictures. Listen to your teacher tell the story.

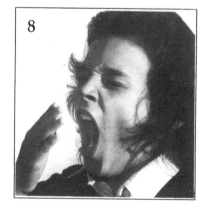

Yawning Is Contagious

CHEN works at a restaurant in the daytime. In the evening he goes to an adult school. He is learning English at the adult school.

This evening Chen's class is reading a story. The story is interesting, and Chen wants to read it. But Chen is tired; he can't read. He yawns loudly.

Sofia is sitting next to Chen. She sees Chen yawn. She yawns, too.

Ali is sitting behind Chen. Ali hears Chen yawn. Ali yawns, too.

Chen is yawning because he is tired. But Sofia and Ali aren't tired. Why are they yawning?

Sofia and Ali are yawning because yawning is contagious. When one person yawns, other people yawn, too.

On this page there is a photo of a woman. The woman is yawning. Look at the photo for 30 seconds. DO NOT YAWN! Ready? Go!

Can you look at the picture and not yawn? Most people can't. When most people look at the photo, they yawn. Yawning is *very* contagious!

2. VOCABULARY

Write the opposites. You can find the words in the story.

1. play   w   o   r   k
2. nighttime   ___ ___ y ___ ___ ___ ___
3. child   ___ ___ ___ l ___
4. teaching   l ___ ___ ___ ___ ___ ___ ___ ___
5. standing   ___ ___ ___ t ___ ___ ___ ___
6. in front of ___ ___ ___ ___ ___ d

3. COMPREHENSION

UNDERSTANDING THE MAIN IDEA

Circle the letter of the best answer.

1. Chen yawns because he is
   a. hungry.
   b. angry.
   c. tired.
2. Sofia and Ali yawn because
   a. the story is not interesting.
   b. Chen yawned.
   c. they are tired.
3. Yawning is contagious. When one person yawns, other people
   a. don't like it.
   b. are afraid.
   c. yawn, too.

REMEMBERING DETAILS

Which sentence is correct? Circle _a_ or _b_.

1. a. Chen works at a factory in the daytime.
    b. Chen works at a restaurant in the daytime.

2. a. In the evening he goes to an adult school.
    b. In the afternoon he goes to an adult school.

3. a. He is learning Spanish at the adult school.
    b. He is learning English at the adult school.

4.   **a.** This evening Chen's class is writing a story.

     b. This evening Chen's class is reading a story.

5.   **a.** Chen is tired; he yawns loudly.

     b. Chen is tired; he talks loudly.

6.   **a.** Sofia and Ali yawn because yawning is interesting.

     b. Sofia and Ali yawn because yawning is contagious.

4. DISCUSSION

How do you say "yawn" in your native language? Can you say "yawn" in your native language five times, and not yawn? Who wants to try it?

5. WRITING

In Chen's class at the adult school, the students are reading a story. What do you do in your English class? Do you read stories? Do you write? Do you practice speaking? Together with your classmates make a list. Your teacher will write the list on the blackboard. Then copy the list here.

In our English class, we

1. _____

2. _____

3. _____

4. _____

5. _____

6. _____

Look over the list. What do you like to do very much? Put a star (*) next to those things.

Now count your classmates. How many people put a star next to 1? _____ How many people put a star next to 2? _____ 3? _____ 4? _____ 5? _____ 6? _____ What do your classmates like to do best in English class?

1. PRE-READING

Look at the pictures. Listen to your teacher tell the story.

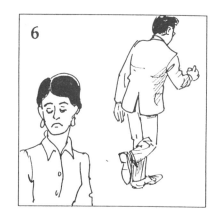

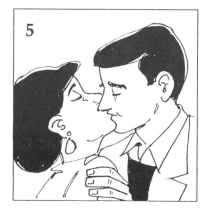

A Love Story

ANNA is talking to her father. "Papa," Anna says. "I'm in love, and I want to get married. I want to marry Iztok."

"Iztok!" Anna's father says. "No! You can't marry Iztok. He's an artist. Artists don't make a lot of money. Marry an engineer. Engineers make a lot of money."

Anna tells Iztok, "I can't marry you. I'm going to marry an engineer."

Iztok is silent for a few minutes. Then he kisses Anna. "OK," he tells Anna. "Marry your engineer. Maybe he can make money. But can he kiss?" Iztok walks away.

Anna marries an engineer. She and her husband have three children. But Anna is not happy with her husband. She thinks about Iztok every day.

Iztok gets married, too. He and his wife have two children. But Iztok is not happy with his wife. He thinks about Anna every day.

Many years later, Anna divorces her husband, and Iztok divorces his wife. Then Iztok and Anna get married. Anna is 45 years old, and Iztok is 51. They are not young. But they are in love. And they are finally happy.

2. VOCABULARY

Write the opposites. You can find the words in the story.

1. mother   _f_ _a_ _t_ _h_ _e_ _r_

2. can   _ _ _ _ _n_'_

3. a little   _ _ _ _o_ _

4. husband   _ _ _ _e_

5. divorce   _ _ _r_ _

6. old   _y_ _ _ _ _

3. COMPREHENSION

REMEMBERING DETAILS

Which sentence is correct? Circle *a* or *b*.

1.   **a.** Anna's father says, "You can't marry Iztok!"
     b. Anna's mother says, "You can't marry Iztok!"

2.   **a.** Iztok is a teacher.
     b. Iztok is an artist.

3.   **a.** Anna marries an engineer.
     b. Anna marries a doctor.

4.   **a.** Anna is happy with her husband.
     b. Anna is not happy with her husband.

5.   **a.** Iztok thinks about Anna every day.
     b. Iztok never thinks about Anna.

6.   **a.** Many years later, Anna divorces Iztok.
     b. Many years later, Anna marries Iztok.

UNDERSTANDING PRONOUNS

Who is it? What is it? Write the letter of your answer on the line.

1. __C__ *He* says, "You can't marry Iztok."

2. _____ *He*'s an artist.

3. _____ *They* don't make a lot of money.

4. _____ *They* make a lot of money.

5. _____ *She* marries an engineer.

a. engineers

b. Anna

c. Anna's father

d. artists

e. Iztok

---

4. DISCUSSION

FOR MEN ONLY: Brainstorm with the men in your class. Describe a good wife. Your teacher will write the words on the blackboard.

FOR WOMEN ONLY: Brainstorm with the women in your class. Describe a good husband. Your teacher will write the words on the blackboard.

---

5. WRITING

FOR MEN ONLY

Look at the words on the blackboard. Which words do *you* think describe a good wife? Copy them here.

A GOOD WIFE

FOR WOMEN ONLY

Look at the words on the blackboard. Which words do *you* think describe a good husband? Copy them here.

A GOOD HUSBAND

1. PRE-READING

Look at the pictures. Listen to your teacher tell the story.

No More Space!

PATRICIA Ball is on vacation from work, but she is not happy. She has only $45. Where can she go with only $45? Nowhere! What can she do with only $45? Nothing!

Then she has an idea. For $45, she can get a tattoo!

She pays $45 and gets a small tattoo on her chest. It is a tattoo of a horse. Patricia likes the tattoo.

A few weeks later, Patricia has some extra money, so she gets another tattoo. It is a rainbow. Patricia likes the rainbow. She wants more tattoos.

During the next ten years, Patricia gets hundreds of tattoos. She gets a Native American on her arm. She gets the ocean on her leg, with green plants and silver fish. She gets a jungle on her back, with green trees, orange birds, and a blue waterfall.

Patricia gets tattoos everywhere on her body; only her face and neck have no tattoos. Patricia wants more tattoos, but she can't have them. There is no more space for tattoos!

2. VOCABULARY

Which colors are in the story? Find them. Write the words under *COLORS*. Then find the words for parts of the body, things in the ocean, and things in the jungle. Write the words on the lines.

COLORS	PARTS OF THE BODY	THINGS IN THE JUNGLE
green	*chest*	
		THINGS IN THE OCEAN

3. COMPREHENSION

REMEMBERING DETAILS

Which sentence is correct? Circle *a* or *b*.

1. a. Patricia pays $450 for a small tattoo of a horse.
    b. Patricia pays $45 for a small tattoo of a horse.

2. a. During the next ten years, Patricia gets hundreds of rainbows.
    b. During the next ten years, Patricia gets hundreds of tattoos.

3. a. Patricia gets a Native American on her arm.
    b. Patricia gets a Native American on her leg.

4. a. She gets a jungle on her leg, with green plants and silver fish.
    b. She gets the ocean on her leg, with green plants and silver fish.

5. a. Only Patricia's face and neck have no tattoos.
    b. Only Patricia's face and back have no tattoos.

REVIEWING THE STORY

Write the correct word on the line.

Patricia is on vacation from work, but she has only $45. Where can she go with

only $45? _____*Nowhere*_____ ! What can she do with only $45?

_____ ! Then Patricia has an idea. For $45, she can get a

_____ ! Patricia likes her tattoo very much. During the next

ten years, she gets _____ of tattoos. Patricia wants more

tattoos, but she can't have them. There is no more _____

for tattoos!

4. DISCUSSION

Circle *yes* or *no*.

1. Some men in my native country have tattoos.	YES	NO
2. Some women in my native country have tattoos.	YES	NO
3. I like tattoos.	YES	NO
4. I like Patricia Ball's tattoos.	YES	NO
5. Maybe someday I will get a tattoo.	YES	NO

In a small group, show your answers to your classmates. Are your answers and your classmates' answers the same?

5. WRITING

Draw some tattoos on the man. Then write about the man's tattoos. For example:

He has a tiger on his chest.
He has a heart on his arm.

Now write your sentences.

_____

_____

_____

_____

1. PRE-READING

Look at the pictures. Listen to your teacher tell the story.

Looking for Love

JOHN is 52 years old. He is not married. Every day he comes home from work and eats dinner alone. Then he watches TV alone. At 11 o'clock he goes to bed alone.

John is not happy. He has a good job and a nice house, but he doesn't have love. He wants a wife.

How can John find a wife? One day he has an idea.

John is a painter, and he drives a small truck. He paints these words on his truck:

> **WANTED — A WIFE**
> **ARE YOU 35-45 YEARS OLD?**
> **DO YOU LIKE CHILDREN, PETS, AND QUIET TIMES? PLEASE WRITE ME.**
> **MY ADDRESS IS 307 S. SIXTH ST.**
> **I AM A HARD-WORKING MAN.**

Hundreds of women write letters to John. He reads all the letters. He likes one letter very much.

The letter is from Bobbi. Bobbi is 33 years old, and she is divorced. She has two children and a dog.

John calls Bobbi, and they meet. One week later, John paints his truck white.

''I'm not looking for love now,'' John says with a smile.

One year later, John and Bobbi are married.

2. VOCABULARY

Write the correct word on the line.

hard-working	pets	alone
nice	calls	meets

1. John doesn't have a wife or children. Every day he eats dinner

    _____*alone*_____ .

2. John's house has three bedrooms and two bathrooms. It has a big kitchen and a

    lot of windows. It's a _____ house.

3. John likes dogs and cats. He likes _____ .

4. John works every day from eight o'clock in the morning to six o'clock in the

    evening. He is a _____ man.

5. John reads Bobbi's letter. Then he goes to the telephone and

    _____ her.

6. When John _____ Bobbi, he says, "Hi. I'm John," and she

    says, "Hi. I'm Bobbi."

3. COMPREHENSION

UNDERSTANDING PRONOUNS

Who is it? What is it? Write the letter of your answer on the line.

1. __b__ *He* is a painter.

2. _____ *It* is 307 S. Sixth Street.

3. _____ John reads *them*.

4. _____ *She* has two children and a dog.

5. _____ John paints *it* white.

a. his truck

b. John

c. John's address

d. the letters

e. Bobbi

REMEMBERING DETAILS

Which sentence is correct? Circle *a* or *b*.

1. (a.) Every day John comes home and eats dinner alone.
    b. Every day John comes home and eats dinner with his family

2. **a.** John has a good job and a nice house, but he doesn't have money.
   b. John has a good job and a nice house, but he doesn't have love.

3. **a.** John is a painter, and he drives a small truck.
   b. John is a repairman, and he drives a small car.

4. **a.** John paints these words on his truck: WANTED—A WIFE.
   b. John paints these words on his truck: WANTED—A JOB.

5. **a.** Ten women write letters to John.
   b. Hundreds of women write letters to John.

4. DISCUSSION

How can people find a husband or a wife? Which ideas are good ideas? Circle *yes* or *no*.

	IS IT A GOOD IDEA?	
1. Put an ad in the newspaper.	YES	NO
2. Tell your parents: Please find a husband (or wife) for me.	YES	NO
3. Tell your friends: Please find a husband (or wife) for me.	YES	NO
4. Go dancing.	YES	NO
5. Go to a church, temple, or mosque.	YES	NO
6. Look for a husband or wife at work or at school.	YES	NO

Now count your classmates. How many people think 1 is a good idea? _____
How many think 2 is a good idea? _____ 3? _____ 4? _____ 5? _____
6? _____ Which idea is best? What do your classmates think? Do they have other good ideas?

5. WRITING

Imagine that you are not married. You are looking for a husband or a wife. You have a small truck. You paint these words on your truck:

WANTED—A _____

ARE YOU _____ **—** _____ **YEARS OLD?**

DO YOU LIKE _____ **,** _____ **,**

AND _____ **? PLEASE WRITE ME.**

MY ADDRESS IS _____ **.**

UNIT **8**

1. PRE-READING

Look at the pictures. Listen to your teacher tell the story.

Sunshine in a Box

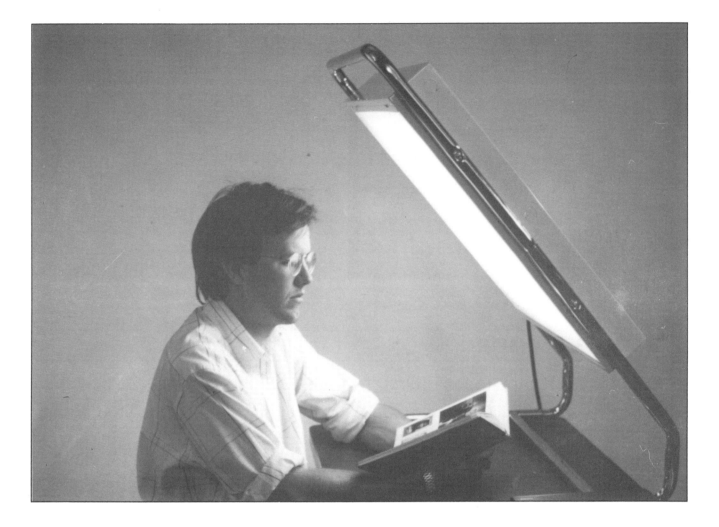

VICTOR is from Guatemala, but now he lives in New York City.

Victor likes New York in the summer, but he doesn't like New York in the winter. He feels terrible in the winter. He gets headaches and stomachaches often. He sleeps too much — 16 or 18 hours every day. He also eats too much. Sometimes he eats 20 candy bars in 15 minutes! And he is always sad.

Why does Victor feel terrible in the winter?

Victor feels terrible in the winter because he needs sunshine. In New York, there is only a little sunshine in the winter.

So, Victor buys a Sunbox. A Sunbox is a big light. In the winter, Victor sits under the Sunbox for two or three hours every day. Then he feels fine. He doesn't have headaches or stomachaches. He doesn't sleep too much or eat too much. He is not sad.

Many people in the North have Victor's problem: They feel terrible in the winter because they need sunshine. So, they buy Sunboxes. They say, ''The Sunbox is sunshine in a box.'' But Victor says, ''My Sunbox is Guatemala in a box!''

2. VOCABULARY

Write the correct word or words on the line.

sunshine   stomachache   headache
candy bars   terrible   North

1. Victor's head feels bad. He has a _____ *headache* _____ .

2. Victor's stomach feels bad. He has a _____ .

3. Victor likes chocolate. He eats _____ .

4. Victor feels very bad in the winter. He feels _____ .

5. In New York the sun doesn't shine much in the winter. There is only a little

   _____ .

6. Guatemala is in the South, and New York is in the _____ .

3. COMPREHENSION

UNDERSTANDING THE MAIN IDEA

Circle the letter of the best answer.

1. Victor feels terrible in the winter because
   a. his family is in Guatemala.
   b. he doesn't like his job.
   c. he needs sunshine.

2. Victor sits under the Sunbox because
   a. the Sunbox shows pictures of Guatemala.
   b. he likes to read every day.
   c. the Sunbox gives Victor light.

REMEMBERING DETAILS

One word in each sentence is not correct. Find the word and cross it out. Write the correct word.

Guatemala

1. Victor is from ~~Germany.~~

2. Victor doesn't like New York City in the summer.

3. Victor gets earaches and stomachaches often.

4. Victor sleeps too little—16 or 18 hours a day.

5. Sometimes Victor eats 2 candy bars in 15 minutes.

4. DISCUSSION

Where is your native city (or town)? Put an X on the map.

Now think about the weather in your native city. Check (✓) your answers.

	OFFEN	SOMETIMES	NEVER
1. It is hot.	_____	_____	_____
2. It is cold.	_____	_____	_____
3. It is sunny.	_____	_____	_____
4. It is cloudy.	_____	_____	_____
5. It is windy.	_____	_____	_____
6. It rains.	_____	_____	_____
7. It snows.	_____	_____	_____

Show your answers to a classmate. Tell your classmate about the weather in your native city.

5. WRITING

Write a few sentences about the weather in your native city. Here is an example.

My city is Jalapa, Mexico. In Jalapa we say: We have four seasons in one day. In the morning it is cold. At noon it is hot. At four o'clock it rains. At night it is cold again. Four seasons in one day!

Now write your sentences on your own paper.

UNIT 9

1. PRE-READING

Look at the pictures. Listen to your teacher tell the story.

Two Happy Men

PEDRO Rossi is happy — he is very, very happy! He won the lottery! He won $500,000!

Pedro is happy for a few minutes. Then he remembers: His lottery ticket! He threw it in the garbage can!

Pedro runs to the garbage can and looks inside. The garbage can is empty!

"Where is the garbage?" Pedro asks his wife.

"The garbage is gone," his wife says. "The garbage truck came this morning."

The garbage truck takes the garbage to the garbage dump. Pedro goes to the dump. He looks in the garbage for two days. He doesn't find his lottery ticket.

Pedro lives in a town in Brazil. Pedro tells the people in the town, "Look for my lottery ticket at the dump. If you find it, I will give you half the money."

Every day hundreds of people go to the dump. They look in the garbage for the ticket. Five days later, a man finds it. Pedro gives the man $250,000.

Pedro won $500,000 in the lottery. Now he has only $250,000. But he is not sad. "Before, one man was happy," Pedro says. "Now two men are happy!"

2. VOCABULARY

Match the words and the pictures. Write your answer on the line.

garbage truck   lottery ticket   garbage can
dump   half   town

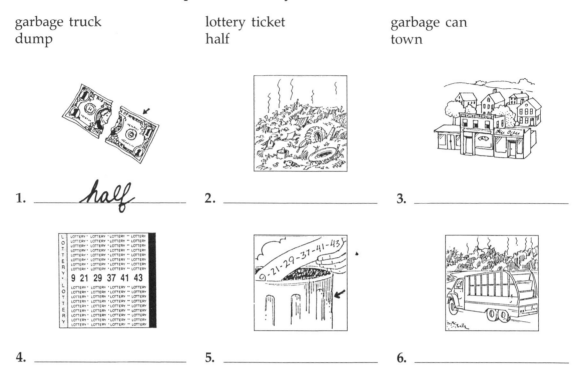

1. ___*half*___   2. _____   3. _____

4. _____   5. _____   6. _____

3. COMPREHENSION

MAKING CONNECTIONS

What is the past tense of the verb? Draw a line to it.

1. is   came

2. win   was

3. throw   won

4. come   threw

REMEMBERING DETAILS

Which sentence is correct? Circle *a* or *b*.

1. a. Pedro won $5,000 in the lottery.
    b. Pedro won $500,000 in the lottery.

2. a. Pedro threw his lottery ticket in the garbage can.
    b. Pedro threw his money in the garbage can.

3. **a.** Pedro lives in a city in Mexico.

   b. Pedro lives in a town in Brazil.

4. **a.** Pedro tells people, "If you find the lottery ticket, I will give you $1,000."

   b. Pedro tells people, "If you find the lottery ticket, I will give you half the money."

5. **a.** A man finds Pedro's ticket at the garbage dump.

   b. Pedro finds his ticket at the garbage dump.

4. DISCUSSION

Imagine this: There is a lottery ticket at the garbage dump in your city. Will you look in the garbage for the ticket? Circle *yes* or *no*.

The lottery ticket is for	Will you look for it?	
1. $100	YES	NO
2. $1,000	YES	NO
3. $100,000	YES	NO
4. $1,000,000	YES	NO

Now count your classmates. How many people will look in the garbage for $100? _____ How many people will look in the garbage for $1,000? _____ For $100,000? _____ For $1,000,000? _____

5. WRITING

Imagine this: You won $500,000 in the lottery. What will you buy? Brainstorm with your classmates. Make a list on the blackboard.

Look at the list on the blackboard. Choose six things that you will buy. Copy the words here.

I will buy

_____

_____

_____

_____

_____

_____

1. PRE-READING

Look at the pictures. Listen to your teacher tell the story.

The Trip to El Palmito

ELENA lives in San Diego, California. Her parents live in El Palmito, Mexico. El Palmito is 750 miles from San Diego.

Today Elena is going to visit her parents. She gets into her flying car. Then she enters "El Palmito, Mexico" into the car's computer.

The flying car goes up into the air. Then it begins to fly. It flies fast — about 350 miles per hour. Elena sits back and relaxes. She doesn't drive the car; the car's computer drives it.

When Elena's flying car is over El Palmito, the car goes down. Elena drives the car to her parents' house. The trip from San Diego to El Palmito was two hours and 15 minutes.

Is Elena's trip to El Palmito really possible? Maybe.

The man in the picture is building a flying car. It is almost finished. The flying car costs $100,000.

So, Elena's trip to El Palmito *is* possible — if she has $100,000 to buy a flying car.

2. VOCABULARY

Match the sentences and the pictures. Write the letter of your answer on the line.

a. Elena *sits back* and *relaxes*.
b. He is *building* a flying car.
c. The flying car is *over* El Palmito.
d. Elena *gets into* her flying car.
e. Elena *enters* "El Palmito" *into the* car's *computer*.
f. The flying car is *almost* finished.

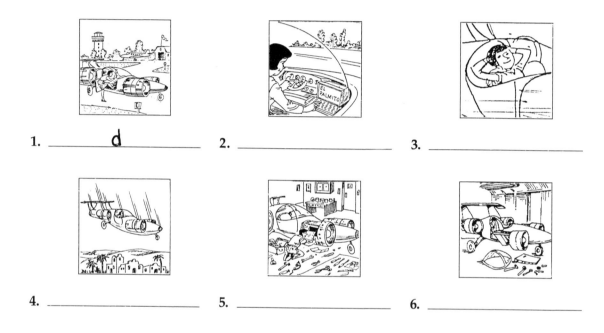

1. _____d_____   2. _____   3. _____

4. _____   5. _____   6. _____

3. COMPREHENSION

UNDERSTANDING PRONOUNS

Who is it? What is it? Write the letter of your answer on the line.

1. __d__ *She* lives in San Diego, California.

2. _____ *They* live in El Palmito, Mexico.

3. _____ *It* is 750 miles from San Diego.

4. _____ *It* drives the car.

5. _____ *It* costs $100,000.

a. the flying car

b. El Palmito, Mexico

c. a computer

d. Elena

e. Elena's parents

REMEMBERING DETAILS

One word in each sentence is not correct. Find the word and cross it out. Write the correct word.

1. Elena is going to visit her ~~sisters~~. *parents*

2. She enters "Miami" into the car's computer.

3. The flying car flies slowly.

4. The trip to El Palmito is about twenty hours.

5. The man in the picture is buying a flying car.

4. DISCUSSION

Where are you now? Put an X on the map. Where do you want to go in a flying car? Put another X on the map.

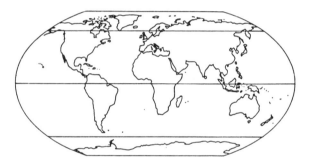

Now look at a classmate's map. Ask your classmate:

· Where do you want to go in a flying car?
· Why do you want to go there?
· What are you going to do there?

5. WRITING

Write the answers to the questions.

Imagine this: You have a flying car. You get into your car.

1. Where are you going? _____

2. Why are you going there? _____

_____

3. What are you going to do there? _____

1. PRE-READING

Look at the pictures. Listen to your teacher tell the story.

A Problem with Monkeys

AN old woman is walking home. She is carrying a bag of groceries. Suddenly a monkey takes the groceries and runs.

Where does this happen? This happens in Hong Kong.

Hong Kong is a big city with a big problem —a problem with monkeys. About 700 monkeys live in a forest near Hong Kong. The monkeys come into the city to eat.

The monkeys take bags of groceries from old women. They take bread from babies. They go into apartments through open windows and take fruit from kitchen tables.

In some apartments the monkeys find cans of beer. They open the pop-top cans and drink the beer.

The people of Hong Kong don't want the monkeys in their city. They say, ''Hong Kong is not a good place for monkeys. The forest is a good place for monkeys.''

But the monkeys don't want to eat in the forest. There is no bread in the forest. And there is no beer!

So, every day the monkeys come into the city. How can people stop them? Nobody knows!

2. VOCABULARY

Which words go together? Connect them with a line.

1.	groceries		pop-top cans
2.	forest		rice, eggs, bread, milk
3.	Hong Kong		animal
4.	monkey		trees
5.	beer		big city
6.	fruit		banana, apple, orange

3. COMPREHENSION

UNDERSTANDING PRONOUNS

Who is it? What is it? Write the letter of your answer on the line.

1. __b__ *It* is a city with a big problem.

2. _____ *They* live in a forest near Hong Kong.

3. _____ The monkeys take *it* from kitchen tables.

4. _____ The monkeys like to drink *it*.

5. _____ *They* don't want the monkeys in their city.

a. the people of Hong Kong

b. Hong Kong

c. fruit

d. 700 monkeys

e. beer

REVIEWING THE STORY

Write the correct word on the line.

Hong Kong is a big _____*city*_____ with a big problem. About 700
1

_____ live in a forest near Hong Kong. They come into the
2

city to _____ . The monkeys take
3

_____ of groceries from old women. They
4

_____ bread from babies. They come into apartments through
5

open _____ and take fruit from kitchen tables.
6

4. DISCUSSION

Are these animals a problem in your native city? Circle your answers. Then show your answers to a classmate. Are your answers and your classmate's answers the same?

Are they a problem?

1. rats   YES   NO

2. cockroaches   YES   NO

3. dogs   YES   NO

4. birds   YES   NO

5. _____   YES   NO
   (write your own)

5. WRITING

Make sentences with the information from the discussion exercise. For example:

We don't have a problem with rats.
We have a problem with cockroaches.

Now write your sentences.

1. _____

2. _____

3. _____

4. _____

5. _____

1. PRE-READING

Look at the pictures. Listen to your teacher tell the story.

The Kind Waitress

EVERY evening at six o'clock an old man goes to a restaurant near his house. He eats dinner. After dinner, he drinks coffee and talks to the people at the restaurant.

The old man's name is Bill. Bill eats at the restaurant every evening because he is lonely. His wife died, and he has no children.

Every evening the same waitress brings Bill his dinner. Her name is Cara. She is 17 years old.

Cara is kind to Bill. She knows he is lonely, so she talks to him. If Bill is late for dinner, she calls him on the telephone. "Are you OK?" she asks him.

One evening Bill doesn't come to the restaurant. Cara calls him, but he doesn't answer the phone. Cara calls the police. "Please go to Bill's house," Cara tells the police.

Later the police call Cara at the restaurant. "Bill died in his sleep," the police tell her. Bill was 82 years old.

A week later, a man comes to the restaurant. "I have something for Cara," the man says. The man gives Cara a check for $500,000. The money is from Bill.

"This money is for me? From Bill?" Cara asks the man.

"Yes," the man answers.

"But . . .why?" Cara asks the man.

"Bill liked you," the man says. "You were kind to him."

2. VOCABULARY

Write the correct word on the line.

waitress   calls   late
lonely   kind   check

1. Bill usually goes to the restaurant at 6:00. One day he arrives at 6:20. Bill is

   _____*late*_____ .

2. Bill has no family, and he lives alone. He is _____ .

3. Cara works at the restaurant. She brings Bill his food. She is a

   _____ .

4. Cara knows that Bill is lonely, so she talks to him. She is

   _____ to Bill.

5. If Bill is late for dinner, Cara _____ him on the telephone.

6. The man gives Bill's money to Cara. It is a _____ for

   $500,000.

3. COMPREHENSION

UNDERSTANDING THE MAIN IDEAS

Circle the letter of the best answer.

1. Bill goes to the restaurant because
   a. the food is very good.
   b. he doesn't like to cook.
   c. he is lonely.

2. Cara talks to Bill because
   a. she knows Bill is rich.
   b. she likes to talk to people.
   c. she knows Bill is lonely.

3. Bill gives his money to Cara because
   a. she was kind to him.
   b. she needs the money very much.
   c. she is his daughter.

REMEMBERING DETAILS

Which sentence is correct? Circle *a* or *b*.

1.   **a.** Every morning an old man eats breakfast at a restaurant near his house.
     b. Every evening an old man eats dinner at a restaurant near his house.

2.   **a.** After dinner, Bill drinks tea and reads the newspaper.
     b. After dinner, Bill drinks coffee and talks to the people at the restaurant.

3.   **a.** Bill has no children.
     b. Bill has three children.

4.   **a.** Cara is 17 years old.
     b. Cara is 37 years old.

5.   **a.** When Bill dies, he gives Cara $500.
     b. When Bill dies, he gives Cara $500,000.

4. DISCUSSION

Bill was lonely, so he went to the restaurant every evening. What can people do when they're lonely? Go dancing? Call a friend on the telephone? Brainstorm with your classmates. Your teacher will write your ideas on the blackboard.

5. WRITING

What about you? What do you do when you're lonely? Write your answers on the lines.

    When I'm lonely, I

_____

_____

_____

_____

_____

1. PRE-READING

Look at the pictures. Listen to your teacher tell the story.

No More Housework!

IT is five o'clock in the evening when Rene Wagner comes home from work. She walks into the living room and looks at her three children. The children are 14, 13, and 9 years old. They are watching TV.

The living room is a mess. There are empty glasses and dirty socks on the floor. There are cookies on the sofa. Games and toys are everywhere.

Rene is angry. "This place is a mess!" she tells her children. "I can't work all day and then do housework all evening. I'm not going to do housework!"

And so, Rene doesn't do housework. She doesn't clean. She doesn't wash dishes. She doesn't wash clothes. Every evening she sits on the sofa and watches TV.

After two weeks, every plate, fork, and glass in the house is dirty. All the children's clothes are dirty, too. Every garbage can is full. The house is a mess.

Then, one day Rene comes home from work and gets a big surprise. The kitchen is clean. The children cleaned the kitchen!

The next day, the living room is clean, and the children are washing their clothes.

Rene tells her children, "OK, I'll do housework again. But you have to help me."

Now Rene and her three children do the housework together. Then they *all* sit on the sofa and watch TV!

2. VOCABULARY

Match the words and the pictures. Write the correct number on the line.

__8__ empty glasses   _____ games   _____ plate

_____ dirty socks   _____ toys   _____ fork

_____ cookies   _____ sofa

3. COMPREHENSION

REMEMBERING DETAILS

Which sentence is correct? Circle *a* or *b*.

1.   a. Rene has one child.
       (b.) Rene has three children.

2.   a. When Rene comes home from work, her children are watching TV in the living room.
       b. When Rene comes home from work, her children are playing games in the kitchen.

3.   a. Rene is angry. She says, "Turn off the TV!"
       b. Rene is angry. She says, "This place is a mess!"

4.   a. Rene doesn't do housework for two months.
       b. Rene doesn't do housework for two weeks.

5.   a. Rene gets a big surprise: Her children cleaned the kitchen!
       b. Rene gets a big surprise: Her friends cleaned the kitchen!

UNDERSTANDING PRONOUNS

Who is it? What is it? Write the letter of your answer on the line.

1. __b__ *They* are 14, 13, and 9 years old.
2. _____ The children are watching *it*.
3. _____ *It* is a mess.
4. _____ *They* are everywhere.

a. games and toys
b. Rene's children
c. the living room
d. TV

---

4. DISCUSSION

What housework do you do? Check (✓) your answers.

	ALWAYS	SOMETIMES	NEVER
1. I wash the dishes.	_____	_____	_____
2. I clean.	_____	_____	_____
3. I wash the clothes.	_____	_____	_____
4. I make the beds.	_____	_____	_____
5. I cook.	_____	_____	_____
6. I empty the garbage cans.	_____	_____	_____

   Show your answers to a classmate. Are your answers and your classmate's answers the same?

---

5. WRITING

What is Rene doing in picture 1? Write your answer on line 1. What is Rene doing in pictures 2, 3, and 4? Write your answers on the lines.

1	2	3	4

1. _Rene is cleaning._ _____
2. _____
3. _____
4. _____

1. PRE-READING

Look at the pictures. Listen to your teacher tell the story.

Alone for 43 Years

T is 1947. In a small town in Russia, some people are talking. They are talking about their leader. His name is Stalin.

"Stalin is not a good leader," a young man says. The young man's name is Ivan.

Suddenly everyone is silent. It is dangerous to say "Stalin is not a good leader." The people look around. They see a policeman. The policeman is listening to them.

Ivan is afraid. "Maybe I will go to prison," he thinks. He runs home. He throws some clothes, some tools, and some pans into a bag. Then he runs into the forest.

Ivan runs for 18 hours. Then he sleeps. When he wakes up, he builds a small house.

Ivan lives in the small house in the forest. He drinks water from a river. He eats rabbits and berries. He is very lonely, but he doesn't go home. He is afraid.

Ivan lives in the forest for 43 years. Then, in 1990, his family visits him. "Come home, Ivan," they say. "Russia is different. Stalin is dead, and Russia has new leaders. It is not dangerous for you now." They give Ivan a newspaper.

Ivan reads the newspaper. "Yes," he says, "Russia is different now."

And finally, after 43 years alone, Ivan goes home.

2. VOCABULARY

Which words go together? Connect them with a line.

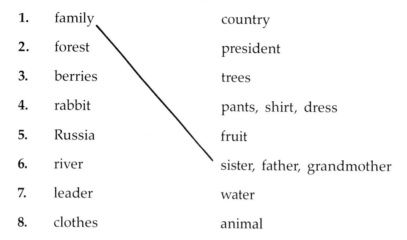

1.	family	country
2.	forest	president
3.	berries	trees
4.	rabbit	pants, shirt, dress
5.	Russia	fruit
6.	river	sister, father, grandmother
7.	leader	water
8.	clothes	animal

3. COMPREHENSION

REMEMBERING DETAILS

One word in each sentence is not correct. Find the word and cross it out. Write the correct word.

1. In a small town in ~~China~~, *Russia* some people are talking.

2. They are talking about Stalin, their friend.

3. "Stalin is not a good leader," a young woman says.

4. It is OK to say "Stalin is not a good leader."

5. Ivan is happy; he thinks, "Maybe I will go to prison."

6. Ivan lives in the forest for 43 days.

UNDERSTANDING SEQUENCE

Which happens first? Write 1 on the line. Which happens second? Write 2 on the line.

1. __1__ Ivan says, "Stalin is not a good leader."

   _____ The people see a policeman.

2. _____ Ivan runs into the forest.

   _____ Ivan throws some clothes, some tools, and some pans into a bag.

3. _____ Ivan builds a house.

   _____ Ivan runs for 18 hours.

4. _____ Ivan goes home.

   _____ Ivan's family gives him a newspaper.

4. DISCUSSION

Imagine that you are Ivan. You are going to run into the forest. But first you go home and get some things. What things do you get? Brainstorm with your classmates. Your teacher will write your list on the blackboard. If you don't know the words in English, draw pictures. Show your pictures to the teacher. The teacher will write the English words on the blackboard.

5. WRITING

Write some sentences about a leader of your country—past or present. Here is an example.

> Queen Isabella was an important Spanish leader.
> She lived from 1451-1504.
> Her husband was King Fernando.
> Queen Isabella gave money to Christopher Columbus.

Now write your sentences.

_____

_____

_____

_____

1. PRE-READING

Look at the pictures. Listen to your teacher tell the story.

The Lawn Chair Pilot

LARRY Walters wants to be a pilot. He wants to fly an airplane. But Larry is not a rich man. He doesn't have an airplane. He has only a lawn chair.

Larry ties 45 big balloons to his lawn chair and then sits in the chair. The lawn chair goes up.

For a few minutes, everything is fine. The view from the lawn chair is beautiful. Larry can see houses and trees below him. He is happy. He is flying!

The lawn chair goes up very high. Larry is afraid. ''I don't want to go very high,'' Larry thinks. ''I want to go down a little.'' With a small gun, Larry shoots 10 balloons. Then something terrible happens. Larry drops the gun, and it falls to the ground. Larry can't shoot more balloons. The chair goes up and up.

Larry is three miles above the ground. Airplanes are flying over him and under him. Larry has a small radio. ''Help! Help!'' he says into the radio. ''I'm flying in a lawn chair, and I want to come down!'' People hear Larry, but they can't help him.

Larry flies in the lawn chair for 45 minutes. Then the balloons begin to lose air. Slowly, the lawn chair comes down, and Larry is back on the ground. He is not hurt.

Larry says, ''For 45 minutes, I was a pilot — the pilot of a lawn chair.''

2. VOCABULARY

Match the sentences and the pictures. Write the letter of your answer of the line.

a. Larry wants to be a *pilot*.
b. The balloons *lose air*.
c. Larry is back on the *ground*.

d. The *view* from the lawn chair is beautiful.
e. With a small *gun*, Larry *shoots* 10 balloons.
f. Larry *drops* the gun, and it *falls* to the ground.

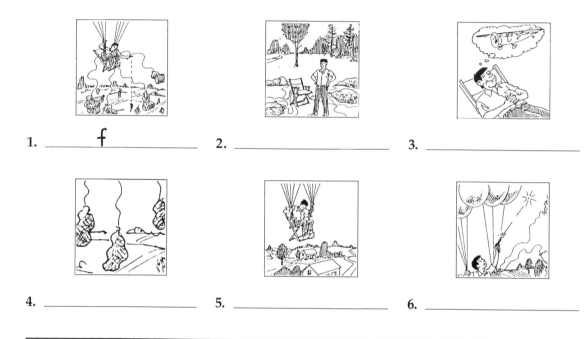

1. _____f_____　　　2. _____　　　3. _____

4. _____　　　5. _____　　　6. _____

3. COMPREHENSION

UNDERSTANDING SEQUENCE

Which happens first? Write 1 on the line. Which happens second? Write 2 on the line.

1. _____ The lawn chair goes up.

   ___1___ Larry ties 45 big balloons to his lawn chair.

2. _____ Larry drops the gun.

   _____ Larry shoots 10 balloons.

3. _____ People hear Larry, but they can't help him.

   _____ Larry says, "Help! Help!" into his radio.

4. _____ Slowly, the lawn chair comes down.

   _____ Larry is back on the ground.

REVIEWING THE STORY

Write the correct word on the line.

Larry Walters ties 45 big ___*balloons*___ to a lawn
_____ and sits in the chair. The lawn chair goes up very
_2_
_____ , and Larry is afraid. With a small gun, he
_3_
_____ 10 balloons. But then he _____
_4_   _5_
the gun, and it _____ to the ground. The lawn chair goes up
_6_
and up.

After 45 minutes, the lawn chair comes down, and Larry is back on the

_____ .
_7_

4. DISCUSSION

Do you want to do it? Circle *yes* or *no*. Then ask a classmate the questions. Circle your classmate's answers. Are your answers and your classmate's answers the same?

Do you want to

	YOU		YOUR CLASSMATE	
1. go up in a lawn chair?	YES	NO	YES	NO
2. be an airplane pilot?	YES	NO	YES	NO
3. ride in a hot air balloon?	YES	NO	YES	NO
4. ride in a spaceship?	YES	NO	YES	NO

5. WRITING

Write your answers to the questions in the discussion exercise. For example:

I don't want to go up in a lawn chair.
I want to be an airplane pilot.

Now write your sentences on your own paper.

1. PRE-READING

Look at the pictures. Listen to your teacher tell the story.

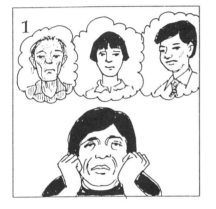

Rent-A-Family

MRS. Sato is sad. It is her birthday, and she is alone. Her husband died in 1985. Her daughter lives in another city. Her son is working.

Mrs. Sato goes to the telephone and calls a company in Tokyo, Japan.

"Hello," a woman answers.

"Hello," Mrs. Sato says. "I'd like to rent a family."

"What would you like?" the woman asks Mrs. Sato. "A son? A daughter? Some grandchildren?"

"I'd like to rent a daughter, a son-in-law, and two grandchildren," Mrs. Sato says.

At seven o'clock that evening, four actors come to Mrs. Sato's house—a woman, a man, and two children. "Happy Birthday!" the actors say. The actors stay with Mrs. Sato for three hours. They talk with her, eat dinner with her, and watch TV with her. Then they go home. Mrs. Sato is happy.

Mrs. Sato was alone on her birthday, so she called Rent-A-Family. Rent-A-Family is a new company in Tokyo. The company sends "families" to people's houses. The families are really actors. The actors visit for three hours. The cost is $1,000.

Most people rent families because they are lonely. Their children and grandchildren don't visit them. But some people rent families because they like the actors. One woman says, "I always argue with my son and daughter-in-law. But I never argue with my rented family. My family is OK. But my rented family is better!"

2. VOCABULARY

Which sentences have the same meaning as the sentences in the story? Circle the letter of your answer.

1. *I'd like* to rent a family.
   - **a.** Rented families are good
   - **(b.)** I want to rent a family, please.

2. What *would* you *like*?
   - **a.** What do you want?
   - **b.** How are you?

3. He is my *son-in-law*.
   - **a.** He is my daughter's husband.
   - **b.** He is my son's friend.

4. I always *argue* with my son.
   - **a.** My son and I talk, and we have different ideas. We are angry.
   - **b.** My son and I talk, and we have the same ideas. We are happy.

5. Rent-A-Family is a *company* in Tokyo.
   - **a.** Rent-A-Family is a building in Tokyo.
   - **b.** Rent-A-Family is a business in Tokyo.

3. COMPREHENSION

REMEMBERING DETAILS

Which sentence is correct? Circle *a* or *b*.

1. **(a.)** Mrs. Sato is sad because she is alone on her birthday.
   b. Mrs. Sato is sad because she is alone on a Japanese holiday.

2. **a.** Mrs. Sato writes to a company in New York.
   b. Mrs. Sato calls a company in Tokyo.

3. **a.** Mrs. Sato says, "I'd like to visit a family."
   b. Mrs. Sato says, "I'd like to rent a family."

4. **a.** At seven o'clock that evening, five actors come to Mrs. Sato's house—three women and two men.
   b. At seven o'clock that evening, four actors come to Mrs. Sato's house—a woman, a man, and two children.

REVIEWING THE STORY

Write the correct word on the line.

Rent-A-Family is a new ___*Company*___ in Tokyo, Japan. The
                                    1

company sends actors to people's houses. The actors visit for three

_____ . The _____ is $1,000.

Most people _____ families because they are lonely. But

some people rent families because they _____ the actors.

They say, "My family is OK, but my rented family is _____ !"

4. DISCUSSION

Mrs. Sato has a son and a daughter. Her son's name is Masao, and her daughter's name is Yuko. Masao is not married, but Yuko is married. Yuko's husband is named Kenji. Yuko and Kenji have two children.

This is the Satos' family tree:

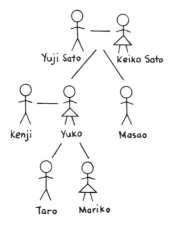

Draw your family tree. Show your family tree to a classmate. Tell your classmate about the people in your family.

5. WRITING

Mrs. Sato lives alone in an apartment in Tokyo. Every day she cleans her apartment, goes shopping, and cooks her dinner. She also watches TV and talks to her neighbors. She is happy, but sometimes she is lonely.

What about you? Where will you live when you are 70 years old? What will you do every day? How will you feel? Complete the sentences.

1. I will live with _____ .

2. Every day I will _____

_____ .

3. I will feel _____ .

UNIT **17**

1. PRE-READING

Look at the pictures. Listen to your teacher tell the story.

The Power of Love

DONNY, an 11-year-old boy, is playing with a ball. The ball goes into the street, and Donny runs for the ball. A car hits Donny.

An ambulance takes Donny to the hospital. The doctors at the hospital tell Donny's parents, "Donny is in a coma. Maybe he will wake up tomorrow. Maybe he will wake up next week. Or maybe he will never wake up."

Every day Donny's parents visit him at the hospital. They sit next to Donny's bed and talk to him. But Donny never talks to them. He just sleeps.

One day Donny's father says, "Wake up, Donny. Wake up and come home. Come home and play with Rusty." Rusty is Donny's dog.

When Donny's father says "Rusty," Donny moves his arm.

"Rusty!" Donny's father says again. Again, Donny moves his arm.

Donny's parents have an idea. They tell the nurses, "We want to bring Donny's dog to the hospital. Is it OK?"

"A dog in the hospital?" the nurses say. "That's very unusual. But, yes, it's OK."

The next day, Donny's parents bring Rusty to the hospital. When they put the dog on Donny's bed, Donny opens his eyes and hugs the dog.

Donny's parents bring Rusty to the hospital every day. One day, Rusty jumps on Donny's bed and scratches Donny's arm. Donny says his first words: "Bad dog!"

After seven weeks Donny is well. He leaves the hospital and goes home. Rusty goes home with him.

2. VOCABULARY

Match the pictures and the sentences. Write the letter of your answer on the line.

a. Donny *hugs* the dog.
b. A car *hits* Donny.
c. Donny is in a *coma.*

d. Rusty *scratches* Donny's arm.
e. An *ambulance* takes Donny to the hospital.
f. Donny *moves* his arm.

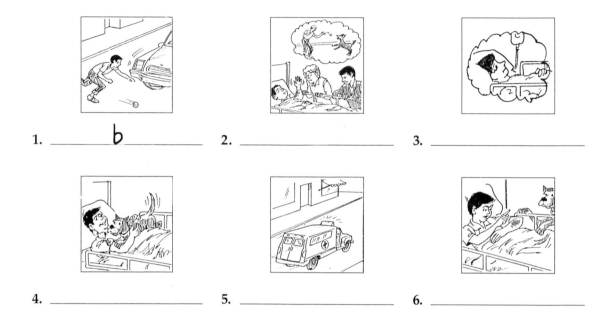

1. _____ b _____   2. _____   3. _____

4. _____   5. _____   6. _____

3. COMPREHENSION

UNDERSTANDING SEQUENCE

Which happens first? Write 1 on the line. Which happens second? Write 2 on the line.

1. _____ A car hits Donny.

   __1__ Donny runs for the ball.

2. _____ Donny's parents visit him at the hospital.

   _____ An ambulance takes Donny to the hospital.

3. _____ Donny's father says, "Come home and play with Rusty."

   _____ Donny moves his arm.

4. _____ Donny's parents bring Rusty to the hospital.

   _____ Donny's parents tell the nurses, "We want to bring Donny's dog to the hospital."

WHO SAYS IT?

Who says it? Write the letter of your answer on the line.

1. _b_ "Donny is in a coma."

2. _____ "Come home and play with Rusty."

3. _____ "We want to bring Donny's dog to the hospital. Is it OK?"

4. _____ "That's very unusual. But, yes, it's OK."

5. _____ "Bad dog!"

a. Donny

b. the doctors

c. Donny's parents

d. Donny's father

e. the nurses

4. DISCUSSION

Donny's father says "Rusty," and Donny begins to wake up from the coma.

Imagine this: You are in a coma. What will wake you up? What smells? What music? Whose voices? What do you need to touch? Brainstorm with your classmates. Think of smells, songs, voices, and things to touch. Your teacher will write your lists on the blackboard.

5. WRITING

Now make your own lists. What will wake you up from a coma? (Maybe there are no English words for some of the things on your list. That's OK; write those words in your native language.)

SMELLS

_____

_____

_____

SONGS/MUSIC

_____

_____

_____

VOICES

_____

_____

_____

THINGS TO TOUCH

_____

_____

_____

1. PRE-READING

Look at the pictures. Listen to your teacher tell the story.

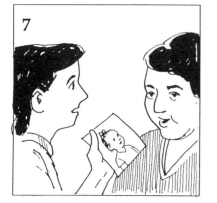

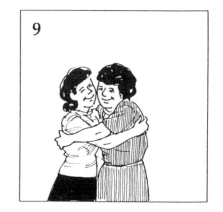

I Think I'm Your Mother

JOYCE is 24 years old. She has a baby daughter, but she can't take care of her baby. The government takes Joyce's baby and gives her to another family.

Joyce never forgets her daughter. For 20 years, Joyce looks for her. She can't find her. She doesn't know her daughter's new name. She doesn't know her daughter's address.

When Joyce is 44 years old, she gets a job at a small store. A young woman works with Joyce at the store. The young woman's name is Tammy. Tammy and Joyce are friends.

One day at work Tammy begins to cry. "What's the matter?" Joyce asks Tammy.

"I feel so sad," Tammy says. "I'm looking for my mother, and I can't find her."

"I don't understand," Joyce says. "I know your mother. She comes into the store sometimes."

"Yes, she's my mother, but she's not my birth mother. I can't find my birth mother because I don't have her name or address. I have only this photo. See? This is me when I was a baby."

Tammy shows Joyce the photo. Joyce looks at the photo for a long time. Then she opens her wallet and takes out a photo. It is a photo of a baby girl. Joyce's photo and Tammy's photo are the same.

"Tammy," Joyce says. "I think I'm your birth mother."

The two women hug for a long time. "This is the best day of my life," Tammy says.

Joyce smiles and looks at Tammy. "This is the best day of my life, too," she says.

2. VOCABULARY

Write the correct words on the lines.

wallet   gets a job   cry
take care of   hug   best

1. Joyce doesn't play with her baby, or wash her, or give her good food to eat.

   Joyce doesn't _____*take care of*_____ her baby.

2. When Joyce is 44 years old, she looks for work.

   She _____ at a small store.

3. Tammy is very sad. She begins to _____ .

4. Joyce has money and a photo of Tammy in her _____ .

5. Joyce tells Tammy, "I think I'm your mother." Then Joyce holds Tammy in her

   arms. The two women _____ .

6. Tammy says, "This is a very, very good day! This is the

   _____ day of my life."

3. COMPREHENSION

MAKING CONNECTIONS

Find the best way to complete the sentence. Write the letter of your answer on the line.

1. The government takes Joyce's baby __*b*__

2. Joyce can't find her baby _____

3. Joyce knows Tammy's mother _____

4. Joyce knows that she is Tammy's birth mother _____

a. because her photo and Tammy's photo are the same.

b. because Joyce can't take care of her.

c. because she doesn't know her address or her new name.

d. because she comes into the store sometimes.

REVIEWING THE STORY

Write the correct word on the line.

Joyce can't take care of her baby. The _____*government*_____ takes the baby and
                                              1

gives her to another family. For 20 years, Joyce looks _____
                                                                    2

her daughter, but she can't find her.

When Joyce is 44 years old, she gets a job at a small _____ .
                                                                    3

A young woman works with Joyce at the store. Her name is Tammy.

Tammy is sad because she can't find her birth _____ .
                                                              4

Tammy shows Joyce a photo. "This is me when I was a baby," she says.

Joyce looks _____ the photo for a long time. Then she
                        5

opens her wallet and takes out a photo. Her photo and Tammy's photo are the

_____ . Joyce is Tammy's birth mother.
          6

4. DISCUSSION

In the story, Joyce opens her wallet and takes out a photo. It is a photo of a
baby girl.

When you left your native country, did you take some photos with you? What
are your three most important photos? Tell a classmate about them. If you have the
photos with your today, show them to your classmate.

5. WRITING

Think about one of your important photos. Then write a few sentences about it.
Here is an example.

*I have a photo of my family. We are standing in
front of our house. It is a beautiful summer day.
We are all smiling.*

Now write your sentences.

_____

_____

_____

_____

UNIT 19

1. PRE-READING

Look at the pictures. Listen to your teacher tell the story.

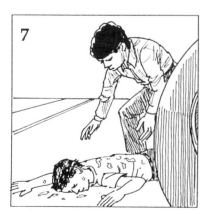

Dear Armando,
Come to the United
States. You can live
with me...

The Escape from Cuba

ARMANDO lives in Cuba. He works in the fields every day. Armando doesn't want to work in the fields. He wants to be an artist.

Armando wants to go to the United States. His uncle lives in the United States. Armando's uncle writes him letters. "Come," his uncle writes. "You can live with me. You can study art."

But how can Armando go to the United States? It is impossible! Only two planes fly to the United States every day. More than 800,000 people are waiting for tickets.

One day Armando goes to the airport in Havana. He sees a big plane. Nobody is near the plane. Armando runs to the plane and climbs up by the wheels.

The plane takes off and flies east. Armando and the plane are going to Spain.

The plane flies high over the ocean. The temperature is −40 degrees Celsius. Armando is wearing only pants and a cotton shirt. He is very cold. He is tired, too. He falls asleep.

Nine hours later the plane lands in Spain. Mechanics are checking the plane when something falls from the wheels. It is Armando! There is ice on Armando's clothes and face. But Armando is alive.

Armando stays in a hospital in Spain for one week. Then he flies to the United States. This time, he flies *inside* the plane.

2. VOCABULARY

Match the words and the pictures. Write your answer on the line.

ticket   airplane landing   mechanic
wheel   field   airplane taking off

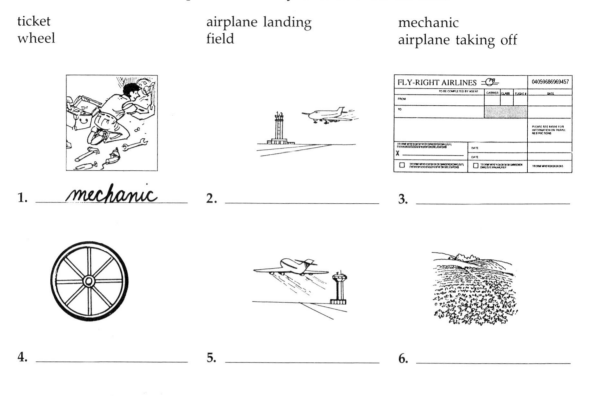

1. ___mechanic___ 2. _____ 3. _____

4. _____ 5. _____ 6. _____

3. COMPREHENSION

MAKING CONNECTIONS

Find the best way to complete each sentence. Write the letter of your answer on the line.

1. Armando lives __d__

2. Armando works _____

3. Armando wants to go _____

4. Armando's uncle says, "You can live _____

5. Armando and the plane fly _____

6. Mechanics are checking the plane when something falls _____

7. There is ice _____

8. When Armando flies to the United States, he flies _____

a. to Spain.

b. inside the plane.

c. from the wheels.

d. in Cuba.

e. to the United States.

f. on Armando's clothes and face.

g. with me."

h. in the fields.

REMEMBERING DETAILS

One word in each sentence is not correct. Find the word and cross it out. Write the correct word.

Havana

1. One day Armando goes to the airport in ~~Lima~~.

2. Armando runs to a plane and climbs up by the windows.

3. The plane takes off and flies north.

4. The plane flies high over the jungle.

5. The time is −40 degrees Celsius.

6. Armando is wearing only pants and a cotton jacket.

4. DISCUSSION

Armando worked in the fields, but he wanted to be an artist. What about you? Do you like your work?

Your teacher will ask you and your classmates: What was your work in your native country? What is your work now? and What work do you want? Your teacher will write your answers on the blackboard in a chart like this one:

NAME	WORK IN NATIVE COUNTRY	WORK NOW	WORK YOU WANT

5. WRITING

Use the information on the blackboard to write about some of your classmates. For example:

−Ding Quan was a teacher in China.
−Miguel is a dishwasher, but he wants to be a cook.

Now write your sentences on your own paper.

1. PRE-READING

Look at the pictures. Listen to your teacher tell the story.

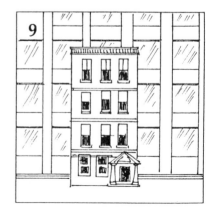

The Cheap Apartment

JEAN Herman lives in an apartment in New York City. Jean's apartment is small, but she likes it. The apartment is cheap; Jean pays only $200 a month.

Jean's apartment is in an old building. One day a big company buys the old building. The company wants to tear down the old building and build a skyscraper.

Some people from the company visit Jean. ''We're going to tear down this building,'' the people tell Jean. ''So, you have to move. Here is a check for $50,000. You can find a new apartment — a big, beautiful apartment.''

''I don't want a new apartment,'' Jean says. ''I like this apartment. I'm not going to move.'' Jean doesn't take the check.

The next day the people come back with a check for $100,000. Jean doesn't take the check. ''I'm not going to move,'' she says.

Every day the people come back with more money. Jean doesn't take their checks.

Finally, the people come with a check for $750,000. ''*Please* take the money and move,'' the people say.

''I'm not going to move,'' Jean says. ''Not for $750,000. Not for a million dollars. Not for ten million dollars. I like this apartment. It's my home.''

Jean doesn't move, and the company doesn't tear down the building. The company builds the skyscraper behind the old building.

And so, on East 60th Street in New York City, there is an unusual skyscraper. The skyscraper has an old building in front of it. Jean Herman lives alone in the old building. Her apartment is small, but Jean likes it. The apartment is cheap; Jean pays only $200 a month.

2. VOCABULARY

Match the words and the pictures. Write your answer on the line.

skyscraper	tear down	old building
move	check	build

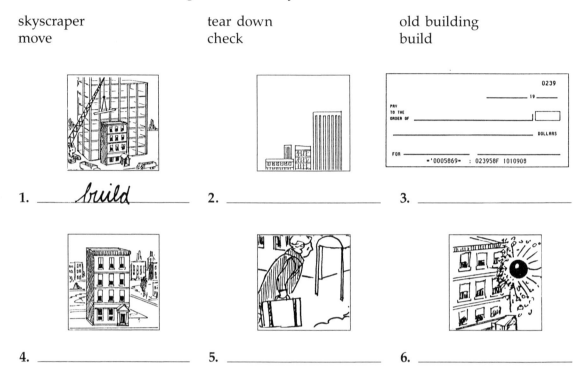

1. _*build*_   2. _____   3. _____

4. _____   5. _____   6. _____

3. COMPREHENSION

UNDERSTANDING PRONOUNS

Who is it? What is it? Write the letter of your answer on the line.

1. __d__ *It* is small and cheap.

2. _____ A big company buys *it.*

3. _____ The big company wants to build *it.*

4. _____ *They* visit Jean.

5. _____ People from the company want Jean to take *it.*

6. _____ *She* lives on East 60th Street in New York.

a. a skyscraper

b. Jean Herman

c. the old building

d. Jean's apartment

e. people from the company

f. a check for $750,000

UNDERSTANDING THE MAIN IDEAS

Which sentence is correct? Circle *a* or *b*.

1.   a.   Jean's apartment is large and expensive.
      b.   Jean's apartment is small and cheap.

2.   a.   A big company wants to tear down the old building and build a restaurant.
      b.   A big company wants to tear down the old building and build a skyscraper.

3.   a.   Jean doesn't take the check for $750,000.
      b.   Jean takes the check for $750,000.

4.   a.   Jean doesn't want to move because she likes her apartment.
      b.   Jean doesn't want to move because she likes New York City.

5.   a.   The company builds a skyscraper behind the old building.
      b.   The company builds a skyscraper one mile from the old building.

4. DISCUSSION

This is the floor plan of Jean's apartment:

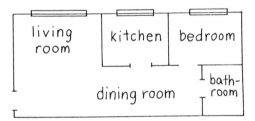

Draw the floor plan of your home (your home here, or your home in your native country.) Show your floor plan to a classmate. Tell your classmate about your home.

5. WRITING

Write a few sentences about your home (your home here, or your home in your native country). Here is an example.

I like our apartment, but it is too small. We have only one bathroom. Every morning we have the same problem: Who will go into the bathroom first?

Now write your sentences on your own paper.

To the Teacher

The original newspaper and magazine versions of many of the Easy True Stories contain information that could not be included on the adaptations because the information would have made the stories too long for beginners or added too many low-frequency words. On the other hand, the information – in many cases, the story behind the story – was just too interesting to leave out entirely. So, it was decided that additional facts would be given here, in a special "To the Teacher" section.

As you will see from the sophistication of the language, this section is not meant to be read by students. Nevertheless, you can transmit the information by other methods: talking about it, acting it out, drawing pictures on the board. You might want to offer the information only if students seem puzzled or curious, or if, in the context of the class discussion, the information would be particularly meaningful. Teachers of beginning students know not to ask for trouble! Also included here are specific teaching tips for the discussion and writing exercises.

Unit 1

THE COLOR TVS

About the Story

The Robbers' List on page 89 is genuine. Two hundred imprisoned robbers were asked which items they preferred to steal. The items are listed in order of the robbers' preference.

Teaching Tips

As a follow-up discussion, you might ask students: Do you have a true story about robbers? The Associated Press reports that 75 percent of U.S. households will be burglarized at least once, so chances are good that students who have lived in the United States for some time will have a true story about being robbed or about someone they know being robbed.

The writing exercise is adapted from "Identification Parade," the activity on page 18 of Christopher Sion's *Recipes for Tired Teachers* (Addison-Wesley, 1985). Sandra Moulding, the contributor of the idea, suggests this prewriting activity: Cut a large picture of a person from a magazine and tape it to the blackboard. Ask students for vocabulary descriptive of the picture.

As students supply words, phrases, and sentences, write them around the picture. If you have time, repeat the exercise with a second picture. Then proceed to the writing activity in the textbook. If you think students might have trouble producing the vocabulary the writing exercise requires, such as *thin*, *beard*, and *glasses*, you can enlarge the four drawings from the textbook on a photocopier and use those drawings for the prewriting activity.

If you prefer to do the writing exercise with the whole class rather than in pairs, cut pictures of people from magazines instead of using the four drawings in the textbook. You will need as many pictures as there are students plus an extra few. Give one picture to each student. Tell students that they saw a robber who is the person in the picture. Tell them to write five sentences about "their" robber. When students are finished writing, collect the pictures, tape them to the board, and number them. Then have students read their descriptions, or you read them, while the other students try to guess which robber is being described.

Unit 2

THE MAN IN THE BLUE CAR

About the Story

The cat on the top of the car was Mrs. Thompson's cat, Panda. Although Mrs. Thompson drove fast in an attempt to elude the man in the blue car, the cat was able to hang on to the luggage rack and survive its adventure unharmed.

Teaching Tips

As a follow-up discussion to the story, you might ask students if anyone has a true story to tell about cats, about being followed, or about driving with something on top of the car.

Unit 3

THERE'S SOMETHING IN THE MATTRESS

About the Story

This true story was abridged so that its length would be appropriate for beginning readers. In the *Easy True Stories* version, Gladys and John share their mattress with a snake for only one night. Actually, they felt something moving in the mattress for quite some time before they decided to cut the mattress open. And the story doesn't end with the discovery of the snake.

The *Morning Call* of Allentown, Pennsylvania reports that Gladys and John sued the mattress company for the trauma and "countless sleepless nights" that the snake caused. The case was settled out of court for an undisclosed amount.

The mattress company does not dispute the fact that there was a snake in the mattress; there were witnesses present when the mattress was cut open. However, the company does not believe that the snake could have entered the mattress during the manufacturing process. How the snake got in the mattress is still, for the company, "a big question."

The couple's attorney scoffs at the suggestion that the couple tampered with the mattress.

The dead snake, which is 26 inches long, is kept in a jar in the office of the couple's attorney.

Unit 4

YAWNING IS CONTAGIOUS

About the Story

Students should have trouble saying the word "yawn" five times in their native language without yawning. According to a report in *Current Science* magazine, yawning is so contagious that talking about yawning or even thinking about yawning initiates yawning. Scientists are not sure why yawning is contagious.

Teaching Tips

In English, to say the word "yawn" mimics the sound one makes when yawning. You might want to call students' attention to that fact, and then ask them to slowly say the word "yawn" in their native languages. Does the word for yawn in other languages mimic the sound one makes while yawning as well?

The writing exercise has a dual purpose. Its primary purpose, of course, is to give students practice writing. It also gives the teacher feedback on which classroom activities students like best.

Unit 5

A LOVE STORY

About the Story

Those of you who are romantics might like to know Iztok's exact words after his farewell kiss. They were: "I dare you to find anyone who will ever kiss you like that for the rest of your life."

Some readers may wonder why Anna* didn't defy her father and marry the man she loved. Anna was only 18 years old, and her father was a European immigrant; she did what she thought a good European girl should do.

Iztok's family, too, was from Europe, although he had lived in South America. Anna told *Parade* magazine, "Iztok knew how to treat a woman, how to share. He had the polish of a European and the fire of a Latin spirit. Every other man I met fell short."

Teaching Tips

You might want to begin the discussion exercise this way: Draw a stick figure of a woman on the blackboard. Label the stick figure "A Good Wife." Then ask the men in the class to describe the qualities of a good wife. As the men in the class supply vocabulary, write their words around the stick figure. Then draw a stick figure of a man and label it "A Good Husband." Elicit vocabulary from the women and write their words around the stick figure. If students have trouble coming up with words, you might want to prompt them with questions, such as *Is she a good cook?* or *Is he strong?*

You might also want to talk about the other issues the story raises: parents choosing their children's spouses; marrying for money; and divorce.

Unit 6

NO MORE SPACE!

About the Story

Over 75 percent of Patricia Ball's body is covered with tattoos. She chose unrelated single designs for her first tattoos, but later decided to divide her body into sections and give each section a theme.

Ms. Ball told The *New York Times*, "This is my way of expressing myself. I have made a complete metamorphosis from caterpillar to multicolor butterfly."

Teaching Tips

Some students who participated in field testing *Easy True Stories* had trouble understanding the story because the idea of a tattoo as an adornment was foreign to them. In their experience, only prisoners in gulags were tattooed. If you think the word *tattoo* might be problematic for your students, you could introduce the story by drawing a tattoo on

---

* Anna's name is actually Marie. In field testing the story, the similarity of "Marie" and "married" caused confusion; consequently, Marie was given the pseudonym *Anna*.

your hand with washable markers or, even better, applying a removable tattoo. You might even put removable tattoos on willing adult students.

You may want to expand on the discussion exercise by asking students their opinions of other things people do to enhance their appearance, such as piercing their ears or noses, perming or coloring their hair, and applying make-up.

Unit 7

LOOKING FOR LOVE

About the Story

John received hundreds of letters from women. What was it about Bobbi's letter that prompted him to contact her?

John told the Associated Press that he liked Bobbi's letter because "she didn't write about herself and her needs and her wants. She told me about her dog and her plants and wrote a paragraph about each of her kids."

Teaching Tips

In the discussion exercise, students are asked if putting an ad in the newspaper is a good way to find a spouse. Some students who participated in field testing *Easy True Stories* said that personal ads were unheard of in their native cities. If your local newspaper runs personal ads, you might want to bring that section to class to show students.

In the writing exercise, students write their own "Wanted – A Spouse" ads. A teacher who field tested *Easy True Stories* in a multilevel class suggests that more advanced students could answer an ad. In a letter to a prospective spouse, they could write a little about themselves.

Unit 8

SUNSHINE IN A BOX

About the Story

It is estimated that millions of people who live in the northern United States suffer from depression in the winter. The depression is often accompanied by other symptoms – a need for more sleep, an increase in appetite (especially a desire for sweet and starchy foods), and a decrease in energy. The clinical name for seasonal depression is "seasonal affective disorder," or SAD. SAD was first identified in the early 1980s.

Parade magazine reports that fewer cases of SAD are found the closer one gets to the equator. Perhaps only 1.5 percent of Florida's population is afflicted, whereas 10 percent of the population of New Hampshire may have SAD to varying degrees. Women with SAD outnumber men seven to two.

Early Sunboxes simply put out light – about one tenth the light that falls on one's eyes on a sunny day. Newer Sunboxes are on timers and mimic a summer sunrise. Sunboxes cost about $400.

It is quite possible that students who come from a sunny climate but who now live in the North, like Victor in the story, may suffer from SAD. If you live in the North, you might ask students if they feel sad in the winter.

Information about SAD is available from the National Institute of Mental Health, Room 15C-05, Department P, 5600 Fishers Lane, Rockville, MD 20857.

Teaching Tips

In the discussion exercise, students talk about the weather in their native cities, and new vocabulary (cloudy, windy, snow) is introduced. You may need to clarify the meaning of these new words before beginning the exercise.

Unit 9

TWO HAPPY MEN

About the Story

Readers may wonder how Pedro Rossi happened to throw his winning lottery ticket in the garbage.

Every morning on his way to work Pedro Rossi stopped at a small store and bought one lottery ticket. He always played the same numbers: 9, 21, 29, 37, 41, and 43. Every evening on his way home, he stopped at the store and checked the winning lottery numbers. Then, when he got home, he threw his ticket away.

One morning Pedro arrived at the store and found out that a clerk had displayed the wrong winning numbers the previous evening. The correct winning numbers were 9, 21, 29, 37, 41, and 43 – Pedro's numbers. When Pedro ran home to retrieve his ticket, he discovered that the ticket was on its way to the town dump.

The truck driver on the Rossis' route told Pedro the approximate area where he had dumped the garbage, but warned him that with tons of garbage arriving daily, it was unlikely Pedro would find his ticket. After two days of sifting through garbage, Pedro went to the local newspaper, the *Pioneiro*. The newspaper put Pedro's story on its front page.

When a 38-year-old mail carrier found the ticket five days later, Pedro discovered that under Brazil's "finder's keepers" law, the mail carrier was entitled to the entire $500,000. The mail carrier, however, elected to keep his end of the bargain and split the money with Pedro.

Unit 10

THE TRIP TO EL PALMITO

About the Story

The flying car is sometimes called a skycar. It is part car, part helicopter, and part jet plane: It drives along city streets, takes off and lands like a helicopter, and flies like a jet plane.

According to the story, the car's computer drives it. It does, but with help from satellites and from air-traffic computers on the ground. The air-traffic computers program the flying car's computer to fly the shortest route to its destination. They also keep it a safe distance away from other flying cars.

Popular Mechanics reports that, initially, a flying car will cost about $100,000. If, however, flying cars catch on, the price will go down – perhaps to the point where a flying car costs no more than a conventional luxury car.

Unit 11

A PROBLEM WITH MONKEYS

About the Story

Zoologists believe that the monkeys are descended from abandoned pet monkeys. At first, the monkeys stayed in the small woods that Hong Kong residents now call Monkey Hill. The monkeys became a tourist attraction and Hong Kong residents came by bus and taxi each weekend to feed them. As a result, the monkeys lost their fear of people. Now, when the tourists do not provide enough food, the monkeys simply go into the city and take what they need.

The *New York Times* recounts the story of one Hong Kong resident who put a bowl of fruit on her dining room table, only to have the centerpiece eaten by six monkeys who climbed inside the house. Another Hong Kong woman says a monkey reached inside her window and tried to grab a piece of bread her child was eating.

Zoologists do not have an easy solution to the monkey problem. They say the monkeys are now getting more than half their food from humans, so that if the monkeys were somehow barred from the city, the woods could not supply enough food for all of them. The only solution may be trapping and killing the most aggressive monkeys.

Unit 12

THE KIND WAITRESS

About the Story

Bill Cruxton ate lunch and dinner at Dink's Restaurant in Chagrin Falls, Ohio, every day. The employees and customers at the restaurant were like family to him. He was especially fond of Cara, a high school student who worked part-time at the restaurant. Cara's father had died, and one waitress told the Associated Press that Bill "felt like he was a father figure."

Although Bill's sister and four other people contested the will, Cara received almost all of the $500,000.

Unit 13

NO MORE HOUSEWORK!

About the Story

Rene Wagner, a single working mom, told the *Daily Sentinel* in Sitka, Alaska, that she was tired of "ranting and raving" to get her children to help with the housework. She said that the hardest thing about refusing to do housework was fighting her strong impulse to jump in and clean up the mess. But she stuck to her guns. When there were no more clean dishes, Rene stopped cooking and went to a restaurant for meals, leaving the children to fend for themselves.

Unit 14

ALONE FOR 43 YEARS

About the Story

In the story, Ivan says Stalin is not a good leader. Actually, Ivan's criticism of Stalin was not quite so blunt. Stalin had denounced an officer under whom Ivan had served in World War II. According to Stalin, the officer had made tactical errors in the closing months of the war. Ivan spoke out in defense of the officer – a dangerous act in the Stalin era.

Ivan's "house" in the forest was little more than a hut. He ate wood rats, birds, fish, and mushrooms, in addition to rabbits and berries.

The *London Times* reports that Ivan was visited from time to time by friends who brought him clothes and food. They did not visit often, however, as Ivan's hut was deep in a remote forest. When he returned home, Ivan was in good health, but weatherbeaten after living so long outdoors.

Teaching Tips

Some students may not know who Stalin was. Nevertheless, that should not significantly hinder their comprehension of the story. In fact, students who are themselves political refugees will understand Ivan's predicament only too well.

It is probably not necessary to provide students with detailed information about Stalin. Should students express curiosity, however, here are a few facts that may be of interest: Stalin was the leader of the Soviet Union from 1929 until his death in 1953. Historians believe that millions died during those years. Political enemies who did not lose their lives were sent to prison or to labor camps. Stalin ordered neighbors to spy on one another, so Ivan's fear that he was in danger for expressing his opinion was well-founded.

In the discussion exercise, students brainstorm to generate a list of things they would take with them to the forest. Students in field-testing had no trouble coming up with ideas – ax, knife, blankets – but didn't know the English words for the items. You might want to give each student five or six pieces of paper and a magic marker. Ask the students to draw pictures of the items they would take along. As students show their pictures to the class, write the words on the blackboard. Finally, tape the pictures next to the words they illustrate.

Unit 15

THE LAWN CHAIR PILOT

About the Story

After his 1982 flight in the lawn chair, Larry Walters told the *New York Times*, "It made America laugh." The Federal Aviation Administration, however, wasn't laughing. The FAA fined Larry Walters $4,000 for four violations: operating an aircraft for which there is no "airworthiness certificate," flying too close to an airport, not maintaining contact with air traffic controllers, and operating his chaircraft "in a reckless and careless manner."

Two jet airplane pilots who spotted Walters estimated that he was flying his lawn chair at an altitude of 16,000 feet.

Unit 16

RENT-A-FAMILY

About the Story

There are a number of rent-a-family companies in Japan. One in Chiba, for instance, is called Japan Efficiency Headquarters. The company in the story is a composite of several companies; for simplicity's sake, it was given the pseudonym "Rent-A-Family."

The Associated Press reports that the emergence of rent-a-family companies in Japan is due in part to a post-war change in Japanese society: Elderly parents often do not live with their oldest son's family, as was almost always the case before the war. Further weakening the tie between parents and their grown children are the long hours the children put in at work.

Rent-a-family companies say business is booming; Japan Efficiency Headquarters, for example, has 80 people on its waiting list. The company's president says, "Our purpose is to fill a hole in the heart."

Not all Japanese are enthusiastic about rent-a-family companies. A Japanese professor who specializes in aging says, "Personally, it is beyond my understanding," and a Japanese sociologist says simply, "It is very sad."

Teaching Tips

As a follow-up to the rent-a-family story, several discussion topics were field tested. The family-tree topic, though only tangentially related to the story, was ultimately chosen because students responded best to it. You might also want to talk to students about a topic more closely related to the story: the relationship between parents and their grown children. In student's native countries, do parents live with their grown children? If not, where do they live? You may wish to put the following chart on the blackboard:

In my native country,	MANY	SOME	A FEW
1. Old people live with their children.			
2. Old people live in their own houses or apartments.			
3. Old people live with other old people.			
4. Old people are alone on their birthdays and on holidays.			
5. Old people are lonely.			

Students may copy the chart, check their answers under the appropriate column, and then compare their responses with a classmate's. Or, you might poll the whole class and record their responses on the blackboard; instead of using checks, use C to record the responses of the Chinese students, V to record the responses of the Vietnamese contingent, and so on.

Unit 17

THE POWER OF LOVE

About the Story

Current Science magazine reports that brain injuries "scramble" electrical connections in the brain and that it takes time for the brain to put the connections back in place. Nurses and doctors use various stimuli to help the brain restore those connections. "We use the patient's favorite smell, song, story, voice – anything," says Dr. Philip Arnold, an expert in brain injuries. In Donny's case, it was hearing his dog's name that triggered the beginning of his recovery. Doctors said that after his release from the hospital Donny faced a year of therapy before he would be back to normal.

Teaching Tips

In the discussion exercise, students are asked to make lists of things that would bring them out of a coma. You might want to introduce the discussion exercise this way: Lean back in your chair and close your eyes. Tell the students, "I'm in a coma. I'm sleeping. Then a nurse puts chocolate under my nose." With your eyes still closed, sniff a chocolate bar. Then slowly open your eyes and say "I wake up!" Now tell students, "You are in a coma. What smells will wake *you* up?" Write the students' ideas on the board under the heading Smells. Encourage the students to name specific smells (e.g., *Wienerschnitzel* as opposed to "food"). Then elicit words under the headings Songs/Music, Voices, and Things to Touch.

Unit 18

I THINK I'M YOUR MOTHER

About the Story

Joyce didn't take care of her baby daughter because she was an alcoholic. She stopped drinking shortly before she got the job at the store.

Tammy had been looking for her birth mother for almost a year. She told the Associated Press that she wanted to find her birth parents because "I felt like I was incomplete. I didn't know whose eyes I had. I didn't know where my big feet came from. I wondered who I looked like."

After she was reunited with Joyce, Tammy looked for – and found – her birth father. She is now looking for two brothers who were adopted by separate families.

Tammy and Joyce lived only two blocks from each other.

Teaching Tips

If students have trouble understanding the concept of "birth mother," you might try this approach, which clarified the idea for students who participated in field testing the story:

Draw a stick figure of a young woman holding a baby. Then tell the students about the woman's situation. (Some suggestions: Her name is Jenny. She has a baby. She is 16 years old. She has no money. She has no husband.) Then draw a stick figure of another woman. Tell the students about her situation. (Some suggestions: Her name is Linda. She is 35 years old. She has money. She has a husband. But she has no children. She wants a baby.) Tell the students that Jenny gives her baby to Linda, and that now the baby has two mothers. Write *mother* under Linda's picture and *birth mother* under Jenny's picture.

In the discussion exercise, students describe three photos they brought with them from their native countries. If your students *are* in their native countries, ask them to imagine that they are going to leave their native countries. Which three photos would they bring with them?

If your students are comfortable speaking English, you might also ask them the following questions: What happens in your native country when a mother doesn't take care of her children? Does the government take them? In your native country, do adopted children sometimes look for their birth parents? Is it difficult for them to find each other?

Unit 19

THE ESCAPE FROM CUBA

About the Story

In 1969, 22-year-old Armando Socarras Ramirez left Cuba in the wheel well of a Boeing 707.

Newsweek reported that doctors at the hospital in Spain were at a loss to explain how Armando survived the flight at the oxygen-thin altitude of 30,000 feet. One doctor speculated that the cold may have slowed down Armando's metabolism and reduced his need for oxygen. An expert in aerospace medicine pointed out that the doors of the wheel well close after the wheels come up. The air pressure inside the wheel well may have been slightly higher than the pressure outside the plane, and there may have been just enough oxygen to keep Armando alive.

The explanation of how Armando survived the cold was also conjecture. One expert suggested that there may have been some residual heat from the brakes and wheels produced by friction during take-off. Perhaps the air inside the wheel well was warmer than the outside air.

Engineers were amazed that the double wheels of the plane did not crush Armando. Evidently Armando was able to twist his body among the cables and wires inside the well in such a way that the wheels did not crush him.

On June 4, 1993, a 13-year-old Colombian boy stowed away in the wheel well of a DC-8 and flew from Bogota to Miami. Like Armando, the Colombian boy survived the flight, but arrived covered with frost. Students who dispute the facts in "The Escape form Cuba" ("He was from Colombia, not Cuba!") might be thinking of this more recent story.

Teaching Tips

In the discussion exercise, students tell you what kind of work they did in their native countries, what kind of work they do now, and what kind of work they'd like to do. Once the information is recorded on the blackboard, you can ask questions based on the chart, for example: *What work did Khaled do in Saudi Arabia?* or *What work does Miguel want?*

The story offers several other follow-up discussion topics. You might, for example, talk to students about their journeys to the country where they are living now. ("Armando came to the United States by plane. The flight was eight hours. He landed in New Jersey. How did you come to the United States? How many hours was your journey? Where did you arrive?") The information could be put on the blackboard in chart format, and you could ask questions based on the chart. ("How did Wantana come to the United States? How long was her journey? Where did she arrive?")

Another topic for discussion related to the story is students' reasons for leaving their native countries. You might introduce the topic by saying, "Armando left Cuba because he didn't like working in the fields. Why did you leave your country?" For a short writing exercise, students could complete the sentence, "I left my country because..."

Armando's dislike of field work suggests yet another topic for discussion. You might put the following headings on the blackboard:

MY NATIVE COUNTRY		UNITED STATES	
LIKE	DON'T LIKE	LIKE	DON'T LIKE

You could then help students generate lists of their likes and dislikes in their native countries and in their adopted country.

Unit 20

THE CHEAP APARTMENT

About the Story

In addition to the building in which Jean Herman lived, a real estate company bought three other brownstones on Lexington Avenue in New York City. The company then owned the entire blockfront between 59th and 60th streets. When Jean refused to move from her rent-controlled apartment, the company decided to renovate Jean's brownstone and proceed around her. The skyscraper now adjoins the brownstone, and a door in the brownstone leads to a store on the first floor of the skyscraper. Ms. Herman complained to the *New York Times* about the headaches of having a skyscraper erected around her, but said she did not regret her decision.

Teaching Tips

In the discussion exercise, students are asked to draw floor plans of their homes in their native countries. You might want to begin by drawing a plan of your own home on the blackboard and labeling the rooms.

Encourage the students to ask questions about aspects of their classmates' floor plan that are intriguing or puzzling – the presence of servants' quarters, for instance, or a large room for bathing.

As a follow-up to the story, you might pose this question to students: A big company wants to buy your house. The company says, "Here is $750,000. Please move." Do you take the money, or do you say, "I'm not going to move. This is my home"?

Answer Key

UNIT 1

Vocabulary
1. driveway 2. drive away 3. robber 4. fix
5. neighbor 6. carry

Remembering Details
1. b 2. b 3. a 4. a 5. b

Reviewing the Story
1. neighbor's 2. carrying 3. repairmen 4. TV 5. robbers

Discussion
THE ROBBERS' LIST (in order of preference)
1. money
2. jewelry
3. stereos, radios, TVs, VCRs
4. cameras
5. antiques
6. computers
7. guns
8. blank checks

UNIT 2

Vocabulary
1. rearview mirror 2. top of the car 3. wave 4. turn left
5. afraid 6. follow

Remembering Details
1. b 2. a 3. a 4. b 5. b

Reviewing the Story
1. man 2. afraid 3. police 4. officer 5. There's 6. gone

Writing
1. Turn right on Fifth Street.
2. Turn left on Park Avenue.
3. Turn left on Sixth Street.
4. Turn right on Center Street.
5. The police station is on the right.

UNIT 3

Vocabulary
1. turn on 2. wake up 3. husband 4. a little 5. new
6. nothing 7. open 8. inside

Making Connections
1. d 2. c 3. e 4. b 5. a

Remembering Details
1. afternoon/morning 2. off/on 3. sees/feels
4. sleeping/moving 5. old/new

UNIT 4

Vocabulary
1. work 2. daytime 3. adult 4. learning 5. sitting 6. behind

Understanding the Main Idea
1. c 2. b 3. c

Remembering Details
1. b 2. a 3. b 4. b 5. a 6. b

UNIT 5

Vocabulary
1. father 2. can't 3. a lot 4. wife 5. marry 6. young

Remembering Details
1. a 2. b 3. a 4. b 5. a 6. b

Understanding Pronouns
1. c 2. e 3. d 4. a 5. b

UNIT 6

Vocabulary
Colors: green, silver, orange, blue
Parts of the Body: chest, arm, leg, back, face, neck
Things in the Ocean: plants, fish
Things in the Jungle: trees, birds, waterfall

Remembering Details
1. b 2. b 3. a 4. b 5. a

Reviewing the Story
1. Nowhere 2. Nothing 3. tattoo 4. hundreds 5. space

UNIT 7

Vocabulary
1. alone 2. nice 3. pets 4. hard-working 5. calls 6. meets

Understanding Pronouns
1. b 2. c 3. d 4. e 5. a

Remembering Details
1. a 2. b 3. a 4. a 5. b

UNIT 8

Vocabulary
1. headache 2. stomachache 3. candy bars 4. terrible
5. sunshine 6. North

Understanding the Main Idea
1. c 2. c

Remembering Details
1. Germany/Guatemala 2. summer/winter
3. earaches/headaches 4. little/much 5. 2/20

UNIT 9

Vocabulary
1. half 2. dump 3. town 4. lottery ticket 5. garbage can
6. garbage truck

Making Connections
1. is—was 2. win—won 3. throw—threw 4. come—came

Remembering Details
1. b 2. a 3. b 4. b 5. a

UNIT 10

Vocabulary
1. d 2. e 3. a 4. c 5. b 6. f

Understanding Pronouns
1. d 2. e 3. b 4. c 5. a

Remembering Details
1. sisters/parents 2. Miami/El Palmito 3. slowly/fast
4. twenty/two 5. buying/building

UNIT 11

Vocabulary
1. groceries—rice, eggs, bread, milk
2. forest—trees
3. Hong Kong—big city
4. monkey—animal
5. beer—pop-top cans
6. fruit—banana, apple, orange

Understanding Pronouns
1. b 2. d 3. c 4. e 5. a

Reviewing the Story
1. city 2. monkeys 3. eat 4. bags 5. take 6. windows

UNIT 12

Vocabulary
1. late 2. lonely 3. waitress 4. kind 5. calls 6. check

Understanding the Main Ideas
1. c 2. c 3. a

Remembering Details
1. b 2. b 3. a 4. a 5. b

UNIT 13

Vocabulary
8—empty glasses 4—dirty socks 2—cookies 7—games
1—toys 6—sofa 3—plate 5—fork

Remembering Details
1. b 2. a 3. b 4. b 5. a

Understanding Pronouns
1. b 2. d 3. c 4. a

Writing
1. Rene is cleaning. 2. Rene is washing the dishes. 3. Rene is washing the clothes. 4. Rene is watching TV. (or, Rene is sitting on the sofa.)

UNIT 14

Vocabulary
1. family—sister, father, grandmother 2. forest—trees
3. berries—fruit 4. rabbit—animal 5. Russia—country
6. river—water 7. leader—president 8. clothes—pants, shirt, dress

Remembering Details
1. China/Russia 2. friend/leader 3. woman/man
4. OK/dangerous 5. happy/afraid 6. days/years

Understanding Sequence
1. 1,2 2. 2,1 3. 2,1 4. 2,1

UNIT 15

Vocabulary
1. f 2. c 3. a 4. b 5. d 6. e

Understanding Sequence
1. 2,1 2. 2,1 3. 2,1 4. 1,2

Reviewing the Story
1. balloons 2. chair 3. high 4. shoots 5. drops 6. falls
7. ground

UNIT 16

Vocabulary
1. b 2. a 3. a 4. a 5. b

Remembering Details
1. a 2. b 3. b 4. b

Reviewing the Story
1. company 2. hours 3. cost 4. rent 5. like 6. better

UNIT 17

Vocabulary
1. b 2. f 3. c 4. a 5. e 6. d

Understanding Sequence
1. 2,1 2. 2,1 3. 1,2 4. 2,1

Who says it?
1. b 2. d 3. c 4. e 5. a

UNIT 18

Vocabulary
1. take care of 2. gets a job 3. cry 4. wallet 5. hug 6. best

Making Connections
1. b 2. c 3. d 4. a

Reviewing the Story
1. government 2. for 3. store 4. mother 5. at 6. same

UNIT 19

Vocabulary
1. mechanic 2. airplane landing 3. ticket 4. wheel 5. airplane taking off 6. field

Making Connections
1. d 2. h 3. e 4. g 5. a 6. c 7. f 8. b

Remembering Details
1. Lima/Havana 2. windows/wheels 3. north/east
4. jungle/ocean 5. time/temperature 6. jacket/shirt

UNIT 20

Vocabulary
1. build 2. skyscraper 3. check 4. old building 5. move
6. tear down

Understanding Pronouns
1. d 2. c 3. a 4. e 5. f 6. b

Understanding the Main Ideas
1. b 2. b 3. a 4. a 5. a

ACKNOWLEDGMENTS

I wish to thank:

■Sergio Barradas, with whom I field tested *Easy True Stories*. In January he was my student, by May he was my collaborator;

■Beth Duncan, ESL instructor at the Arin Adult Learning Center, who introduced me to Sergio and who followed his progress—and mine—with genuine interest;

■My students at the American Language Institute at IUP, who provided examples for some of the writing exercises;

■Linda Ryan and her colleagues at Harrisburg Area Community College and at Catholic Charities, who field tested *Easy True Stories* and then offered invaluable comments;

■Faye Schirato, ESL Program Manager for Immigration and Refugee Services, Catholic Charities, who made practical suggestions for making the stories and exercises clearer;

■Sharron Bassano, Santa Cruz Adult School, who read an early draft of the manuscript and who helped keep the *Easy True Stories* truly easy;

■Randee Falk, whose editorial marks always make sense;

■Debbie Sistino at Longman, who kept the project moving along;

■Nik Winter, production editor, who skillfully guided the book through its final stages;

■Joanne Dresner at Longman, whose enthusiasm for *True Stories* has not waned after four books;

■Twyla Thompson, who was followed by the man in the blue car, and John Koehler, who advertised for a wife. Thank you for steering me to the right newspapers;

■Nancy Pontier, who told me about the couple who found a snake in their mattress;

■David Venditta at the *Morning Call*, who sent clippings about the snake in the mattress;

■Leon Prudoff of Sleeping Beauty Furniture Mart in Indiana, PA, who donated the mattress for the photo for "There's Something in the Mattress";

■Judy Moyer at the *Olean Times Herald*, who tracked down the photo of John and Bobbi;

■Todd Harden at the National Institute of Mental Health, who sent photos of Sunboxes;

■Paulo Caselani at the *Pioneiro*, who sent clippings for "Two Happy Men";

■Gil Miranda, who translated material for "Two Happy Men";

■Jack Connell, who posed as the man who gave his TV to robbers, and Jessica Kebbe, who posed as the waitress who inherited $500,000;

■Thad Poulson at the *Sitka Sentinel*, who sent clippings about the mom who went on strike;

■Nancy Hayward, who told me about the rent-a-family phenomenon;

■Yoko Gebhard, who offered suggestions for the rent-a-family story.

PHOTO CREDITS

We wish to thank the following for providing us with photographs:

Unit 1
The Color TVs
Sandra Heyer

Unit 2
The Man in the Blue Car
Monterey Peninsula Herald

Unit 3
There's Something in the Mattress
Sandra Heyer

Unit 4
Yawning Is Contagious
A. T. McPhee/Weekly Reader Corporation

Unit 5
A Love Story
Gary Bogdon

Unit 6
No More Space
NYT Pictures

Unit 7
Looking for Love
Olean Times Herald

Unit 8
Sunshine in a Box
Courtesy of the National Institute of Mental Health

Unit 9
Two Happy Men
Courtesy of *Pioneiro*

Unit 10
The Trip to El Palmito
Terrence McCarthy/NYT Pictures

Unit 11
A Problem with Monkeys
South China Morning Post

Unit 12
The Kind Waitress
Sandra Heyer

Unit 13
No More Housework!
James Poulson/*National Enquirer*

Unit 14
Alone for 43 Years
Sovfoto

Unit 15
The Lawn Chair Pilot
AP/Wide World News

Unit 16
Rent-a-Family
AP/Wide World News

Unit 17
The Power of Love
Melanie Stengel/*New Haven Register*

Unit 18
I Think I'm Your Mother
Cindy Pinkston/*Roanoke Times and World News*

Unit 19
The Escape from Cuba
The Bettmann Archive

Unit 20
The Cheap Apartment
AP/Wide World News